TECHNOLOGIES

Understanding type
for desktop publishing

Also from Blueprint

Electronic Publishing Perspectives

Blueprint Dictionary of Printing and Publishing

Word Processor to Printed Page

Desktop Design – Getting the Professional Look

Making Electronic Manuscripts

Publisher's Guide to Desktop Publishing *fourth edition*

Multilingual Dictionary of Printing and Publishing Terms

Blueprint Electronic Publishing Glossary

Typesetting and Composition *second edition*

Paul Luna

Understanding type

for desktop publishing

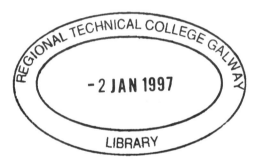
BLUEPRINT
An Imprint of Chapman & Hall

London · New York · Tokyo · Melbourne · Madras

Published by Blueprint, an imprint of Chapman & Hall, 2–6 Boundary Row, London, SE1 8HN

Chapman & Hall, 2–6 Boundary Row, London, SE1 8HN, UK

Blackie Academic & Professional, Wester Cleddens Road, Bishopbriggs, Glasgow, G64 2NZ, UK

Van Nostrand Reinhold Inc., 115 5th Avenue, New York NY10003, USA

Chapman & Hall Japan, Thomson Publishing Japan, Hirakawacho Nemoto Building, 6F, 1-7-11 Hirakawa-cho, Chiyoda-ku, Tokyo 102, Japan

Chapman & Hall Australia, Thomas Nelson Australia, 102 Dodds Street, South Melbourne, Victoria 3205, Australia

Chapman & Hall India, R. Seshadri, 32 Second Main Road, CIT East, Madras 600 035, India

First edition 1992

© 1992 Paul Felix John Luna

Printed in Great Britain at the University Press, Cambridge

ISBN 0 948905 76 X

A catalogue record for this book is available from the British Library

Library of Congress Cataloging-in-Publication data available

Preface

Clarity in printed communication is needed more than ever before. Desktop publishing offers standards of typesetting far superior to those of typewriters and word processors, but also presents users with a hitherto unimagined range of choices – of typeface, of size, of arrangement. This book is aimed at helping you make those choices in an informed way.

The first part provides some basic principles of typography, concentrating on the composition of clear, readable text rather than on the creation of catchy designs. The second part will guide you through the range of typefaces available for desktop publishing by grouping them according to style and use. Apart from a few historical illustrations and reproductions of printed items, all the text and examples were created using dtp applications.

I wish to thank the following who helped me in the writing and production of this book: Charlotte Berrill and Vivien James who commissioned it and, as importantly, made sure that I delivered it; Rob Waller and John Waś who made many suggestions for improvements, and who respectively designed the cover and copy-edited the text; Ruth Grimes who accurately data-captured my longhand; Alan Shelley of Linotype-Hell Ltd., Stuart Jensen of FontWorks UK, Veronika Elsner of Elsner & Flake Designstudios, Andrew Boag and Chris Burke of Monotype Typography, and R. Avard of the Department of Transport who all generously provided information, advice, and material for illustrations; and Martin Slade, director of printing services at Oxford University Press, who oversaw the high-resolution output of the text.

Sources of illustrations

6 (*all*) Department of Transport. Crown copyright.

7 Winifred Beechey, *The Reluctant Samaritan* (1991). Oxford University Press.

8 *The Pocket Oxford Dictionary* (1992). Oxford University Press.

9 The Revised English Bible (1989). Cambridge University Press/Oxford University Press.

11 Alison Black, *Publishing Guide and Glossary* (1991). The Monotype Corporation plc.

18 Laserquill of Windsor.

19 (*top*) Karl Klingspor, *Über Schönheit von Schrift und Druck* (1949). D. Stempel AG.
(*bottom*) José Mendoza, drawing for Photina. Monotype Typography.

20 (*all*) Monotype Typography.

25 (*bottom right*) Adobe Systems Ltd.

71 (*both*) Geoffrey Dowding, *An Introduction to the History of Printing Types* (1961). Ernest Benn.

72 (*both*) John Lewis, *Printed Ephemera* (1962). W. S. Cowell.

73 (*left*) William S. Peterson, *The Kelmscott Press* (1991). Oxford University Press

73 (*right*), 74, 75 Herbert Spencer, *The Visible Word* (1969). Lund Humphries.

The chart on p. 33 is based on one devised by Alison Black in *Typefaces for Desktop Publishing* (1990), ADT Press.

The illustrations on pp. 45, 48 are by Russell Birkett/Information Design Unit.

The typeface listing at the end of the book was produced with the assistance of FontWorks UK.

Sources of quotations

Theodore Low De Vinne, *Correct Composition* (1904) 98–9

W. A. Dwiggins, *Layout in Advertising* (1928) 39 (*top*), 49, 122–3

Camilla Gray, *The Russian Experiment in Art*, Thames & Hudson (1962) 116–20

Hart's Rules for Compositors and Readers at the University Press Oxford, Oxford University Press (1983) 80

James Joyce, *Ulysses* 92, 94–5

Notes to Authors, Chapman & Hall 85–6

Notes to OUP Authors, Oxford University Press 94 (*bottom right*), 101 (*bottom left*), 102 (*bottom right*)

Notes to OUP Authors, Oxford University Press 94 (*bottom right*), 101 (*bottom left*), 102 (*bottom right*)

Robert Louis Stevenson, *Treasure Island* 93, 101, 103

Notes to OUP Authors, Oxford University Press 94 (*bottom right*), 101 (*bottom left*), 102 (*bottom right*)

The Times (9 October 1972) 107–9 (first paragraph in each example)

Walter Tracy, paper to ATypI congress on newspaper design (1971) 102 (*top right*)

Jan Tschichold (trans. Ruari McLean), *Asymmetric Typography* 39 (*bottom*), 47 (*top*)

Virginia Woolf, *To the Lighthouse* 110–15

Contents

Contents

Part I

Understanding type

1

What is typography?

The user of any desktop publishing software becomes a user of the typographic repertoire of typefaces, type sizes, and layout styles. These options and variations are not there merely for aesthetic or stylistic reasons. Correctly handled, the building blocks of typography can make communication work more effectively. Misused, they can give an amateurish or muddled result.

Seeking out ground rules for effective typographic communication may seem a daunting task, but consider the typographic encounters a day may bring. You may have absorbed the news from your newspaper, been pleased to receive a wedding invitation, looked up a number in the telephone directory, followed directions from a road sign, checked spellings in a dictionary, looked up a quotation in the Bible, relaxed with a novel on the way home.

It is a safe bet that you can identify each item listed above by its appearance, and know how to read it because you have become familiar, through use, with its typographical conventions. Looking at some of these typographic forms will bring out some underlying principles of typography which directly relate to its role of communicating the structure and status of information.

It would be wrong to take the examples given here as the only way of designing these particular items – they are far from perfect. But they do show how attuned we are to the genres which typographers have developed to deal with certain kinds of text. Studying existing printed matter is a way of investigating the effectiveness of different typographic concepts, as design survivals have stood the toughest empirical test of all – the ordinary reader.

The newspaper

The newspaper page is a mosaic of text elements. The reader does not wish to read every word, just the stories he is interested in. Newspaper typography has developed a system of signalling items to guide the reader through sections and pages, and to identify individual stories.

Key signals are section and page headings and numbers, the date, and most importantly, headlines. These are differentiated by size and weight to give a sense of the scale of values applied by the newspaper to its stories. Text is relatively undifferentiated – one size is usual for all news items, perhaps with a larger size for the introductory paragraphs. The page is built upon a multi-column grid which enables the news items to occupy rectangles of varying size.

Readers are aware of the kind of newspaper they are reading from a variety of typographical cues. In Britain and the US size is the determining factor: tabloids are racy, broadsheets serious. But more subtle differences lie in the detail of their typography, which reflects their journalistic styles. A serious newspaper may have large, bold headlines, but its text paragraphs will be lengthier than in a more popular paper. A newspaper can be placed on a scale of seriousness by the degree to which text is broken up into short snippets of reading. Page layout differs, too: serious papers try to make each page look regular and well ordered, while tabloids try to look as if everything has been thrown together in an excited rush. (In fact, the tabloid look is carefully contrived.)

What is typography

INTERNATIONAL NEWS

Dole narrows the gap on hesitant Vice-President

Rivals go for the kill as Bush falters

Members of the First Lancashire Fusiliers tend their wounded

Michael White in Nashua, New Hampshire

MR GEORGE Bush set out straight after breakfast yesterday on an unscheduled and decidedly unorthodox whistle-stop tour through southern New Hampshire in an increasingly urgent attempt to stave off fresh disaster in next Tuesday's critical Republican primary.

Before plunging into cookie-nibbling forays in shopping precincts and Main Streets from Nashua to the Portsmouth shoreline, he denounced the Democrats as the "gloom and doom 'Midnight in America' crowd" and declared: "I am taking my case to the people. I understand this state. I come from nearby here and I think I can win it."

It was hardly a clarion call from the front-runner. And Mr Bush's new regional "I'm one of you" theme seemed an inept attempt to hijack Senator Bob Dole's "I'm one of you" slogan in the Midwest. Sounding increasingly confident, the Senate minority leader and his team are now serving BurgerKing hamburgers for the television cameras.

With overnight opinion polls showing Senator Dole, the victor in the Iowa caucuses, closing the gap to within four percentage points of Mr Bush, the race to the White House is suddenly acquiring a momentum which is both rapid and — to a good half of the 13 runners — unsentimentally cruel.

On the Democrat side, little time has been found to acknowledge the enormity of Mr Gary Hart's collapse, from front-runner when he rejoined the race in December, to bottom place today.

Congressman Richard Gep-

hardt of Missouri is, meanwhile, bouncing up in the polls here on the strength of his New Hampshire win, doubling his strength from a pre-Iowa 12 per cent to 21 in one poll, from 8 to 18 in another.

He is showing an energy and killer instinct lacking in Governor Mike Dukakis of Massachusetts this week. "The Duke" retains a large, if falling, lead, with 37 or 35 per cent support among Democrats.

But the smell of blood — Mr Bush's — is suddenly keenest in the camps of Senator Dole and Rev Pat Robertson, the TV evangelist who has metamorphosed into a successful entrepeneur whose product happens to be religion, and who can draw on "a cadre" of five million supporters, not only to win the White House in 1988, he now boasts, but to take the Democrat-dominated House of Representatives in 1988.

It is a racing certainty that Mr Robertson, trailing here, cannot get the nomination or be elected President, but he can help finish off Mr Bush and his "lack of vision."

Coupled with Senator Dole's hard-hitting, almost macho TV ads about being the tough manager of the Reagan successes ("George Bush had nothing to do with it"), this is what brought the Vice-President hurrying from Washington early.

On Wednesday night he joined his five rivals at a chaotic Nashua Republican forum he had intended to ignore. Rather pathetically, his campaign had earlier pulled a rare photo of his weekly lunch with the President which the discreetly pro-Bush White House had given out.

While Mr Dole talked toughness and experience, Mr Bush mixed conscious efforts to do so with a feyness best caught by his reference to the Alaska oil pipeline as something "the Car-

ibou love. They rub up against it and have babies."

Discussing his role in thwarting the nuclear freeze movement, he said: "I will never forget being stoned (laughter), literally stoned, stones being thrown at you, in Germany by the darndest-looking group of radicals you ever saw." The remark recalled the incident when wealthy Mr Bush explained an earlier defeat by Mr Robertson in terms of his Iowa supporters being too busy with "their daughters' coming-out parties" — a social habit commoner in the upper class East than in Iowa.

Whether the problem is being loyally claimed to a fading regime — the snare which has prevented every sitting VP from being elected President since 1836 — or the perception of rich George Bush, the decent but weak yes-man, defeat or narrow victory here would finish him.

In his Concord HQ yesterday confidence still prevailed. "We leapt up 25 points after winning in Iowa in 1980 and fell back again. It's all puff and headlines," said staffer Mr David Calhorn. In Goffstown, a student, Mr David Van Hoof, still confirmed the ironical power of Reaganism which pollsters detect in young voters. "I'm leaning towards Bush because I feel more comfortable, more secure with no change," he said.

But at that time there was still a four-week gap between Iowa and the "Granite State" contest, not eight short days.

The ABC-Washington Post poll yesterday put Mr Bush at 33 per cent (before Iowa he was at 34), Senator Dole at 29 (27) and Representative Kemp at 12 (13) against Mr Robertson's 9 per cent (6) in a state where fundamentalism is weaker and primaries less susceptible to organised entryism than caucus systems.

Over the top again restage battle of th

Paul Webster in Peronne

IT WAS the worst disaster in British military history. The offensive begun by Haig on July 1, 1916, ended four months later with 420,000 British casualties and no tangible results.

A generation died, marching line abreast, carrying 66lbs of equipment per man, up against the German machineguns. In 1918, the British Army limped away from the battlefields of the Somme, leaving its dead behind, taking its memories.

Seventy years later, in Armistice year, there is still little in this bleak landscape, scraped flat for war, to indicate the acres of tombstones set out in rigid divisions or hidden in tiny platoons along forgotten paths. Apart from the occasional restored trench or a local battle panorama, the Somme is more easily evoked among millions of souvenirs in the Imperial War Museum in London or in Canberra, Ottawa, or Pretoria.

Now the Somme departmen-

tal council at Amiens has decided to make up for the years of neglect by creating a research museum, the Historial de la Grande Guerre, largely hinging on the British role in the battle. The decision has political undertones. France faces a series of national and local elections and, as one official put it, "something had to be done for the depressed areas of the eastern Somme."

The home for the new £4 million museum, Peronne, a town of 10,000 people with a Communist mayor, is just off the A1 motorway to Paris, making it a catchment area for the British driving off the ferry or, soon, out of the tunnel shuttle.

In Normandy, the battles following D-Day have long been a huge local tourist business with Caen currently crowning a chain of museums. Now the Somme, too, is looking to the past for present-day prosperity.

The exhibits, which concentrate as much on the build-up to the war as on the battles, are eloquent of the way the p

---

Bill for new weapons may cut strength of US army

George Wilson in Washington

A FALL in the strength of the US army to a 10-year low of 772,600 soldiers this budget year, and a possible drop to pre-Korean War levels, to free money needed to pay for weaponry ordered during the boom days of President Reagan's defence buildup, was forecast by army leaders yesterday.

Mr James Ambrose, who leaves his post as army undersecretary this month, said that, if zero-growth defence budgets continue, as seems likely, he would rather let the army have as few as 521,000 soldiers than try to field a large force without arms needed to combat the Soviet threat.

With money saved through personnel cuts, Mr Ambrose said, he would keep buying

"The idea is to keep people off the battlefield, to keep them alive," he said.

"I don't even know whether the successor to the M-1 tank should be a tank," the former aerospace executive said.

"The first robotic vehicle that the army put on the field was in World War I. Caterpillar (tractor company) made one that was driven by field wire. It's been feasible all that time."

He said that steady decreases in manpower must be accompanied by changes in tactics, such as robot infantrymen and radio-controlled armored cars and aircraft.

It will take a 20-year effort to persuade army leaders to devise ways to fight with fewer men, Mr Ambrose predicted.

His preference for hardware over manpower conflicts with the views of many generals, who have complained that the

million in 1952, and the Second World War high of 5.98 million in 1945.

The proposed reduction this year to 772,600 active-duty men and women would bring the army to its lowest strength since the 758,000 under arms in 1979.

The air force, navy, and marine corps are also cutting manpower as part of the retrenchment ordered by the Defence Secretary, Mr Frank Carlucci, to absorb $33 billion in cuts decreed in a budget summit with Congress last year.

The fiscal 1989 budget to be unveiled next week is expected to reveal only the first part of the biggest military retrenchment since President Reagan took office in 1981, Defence Department officials said.

Unless Congress reverses course on defence appropriations, Mr Reagan's successor

---

Government is 'p Waldheim to resi

Misha Glenny in Vienna

SPECULATION grew in Vienna yesterday that the two partners in Austria's governing coalition, the socialist SPO and the conservative OVP, are bringing pressure on President Kurt Waldheim to resign.

Government sources said

terday that the report of the commission had undermined Dr Waldheim's authority.

This represents a marked shift in Dr Kukacka's position. He has maintained until now that those parts of the report which incriminate Dr Waldheim can be ignored.

The leading conservative daily, Die Presse, published a report yesterday suggesting

What is typography?

THE GUARDIAN
Friday February 12 1988

the First World War

niens as the Fr
nme

George Wilson in Washington

George Wilson in Washington

A grid underlies the pages of all books, newspapers, and magazines. At its simplest it is a series of columns of equal width, but more complex grids allow for columns to be combined to give space for illustrations or wider spans of type. The London *Guardian* uses a strict modular grid where all news stories and photographs fall into a rigid pattern of rectangles. Creating a grid is the first step towards creating order on a typographically busy page.

Headlines are not the only bold items in newspapers: journalists' names are also prominently set. The first issue of the redesigned London *Guardian* (*shown left*) set these bylines in a light weight of type; a stronger style has subsequently been implemented, presumably at the journalists' insistence.

The typefaces used for signalling in a newspaper are relatively strong, ranging from the heavy, simple typefaces of the tabloids to those with a more sophisticated appearance for more serious newspapers. There is generally little white space between letters and words, and the typefaces are chosen to work well when crammed together.

Text typefaces used on newspapers are usually smaller than in books. Although small, they need to appear comfortable to read, and they are often quite narrow to pack in the maximum number of words per line. Newspapers are produced at great speed, and by printing processes which tend to iron out the subtleties of a typeface in small sizes. Newspaper typefaces are not 'rough and ready' but carefully designed to stand up to this treatment and remain legible. All newspapers lay great stress on consistency of typographic treatment, defining the typefaces and sizes of headlines exactly, to ensure that their visual identity is carried forward from day to day.

Typefaces are designed for impact at large sizes or for easy reading of continuous text. The same typeface may not be successful at both tasks.

REDHILL
READING
Reading
Redhill

Words set in an all-capital style all fit into rectangles; words in upper and lower case have more individual profiles.

The road sign

The design of road traffic signs is enforced by legislation, because they must be unambiguous in meaning and instantly distinguishable from competing visual information.

British road signs use only one typeface, a specially developed sans serif alphabet designed by Kinneir Associates in 1962. It is used in upper and lower case (capitals and small letters) because this makes it easier to recognize the profiles of words.

The planning of a directional sign starts with the choice of type size, dictated by the speed of approaching motorists; no variation in the vertical and horizontal spacing of either lettering or directional arrows is allowed.

Recognition of an individual word is sometimes more important than ease of continuous reading.

Transport Alphabet includes specifications for the exact spacing between letters: this is important as too little space will make characters run together when viewed from a distance, and too much space will destroy the word profile.

Three books: a novel, a dictionary, and a Bible

Book typography is not a single discipline, and the design aspects of the following three pages are quite varied.

The design of the **novel** page assumes that the reader simply wishes to identify the chapter and get on with reading the story. The style of chapter opening can be simple or decorative: it does not have to clamour for attention in the style of a newspaper headline. There is very little obvious variation of style within the text: prose and direct speech are presented in paragraphs, conventionally indented. The page number at the foot of the page is unobtrusive, but it reinforces the symmetry of the page. Typefaces for both headline and text do not show any economy, indeed seem to have been selected to fill the page with as few words as possible.

The book designer should choose a typeface with a 'tone of voice' that suits the text. This is a matter of considerable subtlety, and the range of typefaces in which books are designed is relatively (and correctly) conservative. Obviously decorative typefaces may initially seem appropriate for, say, a piece of romantic prose, but excessive prettification soon palls in extended reading. The fancy italic *T* in the headline and the unusual brackets around the page number are the only expressive flourishes in the design. The designer's effort has gone into producing an unobtrusive but appropriate page.

The space on a page is as important as the type. Getting the amount of space between the lines of type right is the first step towards a well-designed page.

The Reluctant Samaritan

supposedly in your wife's absence—saying you had no idea where your wife was and you did not want to hear about her mother or to see her.'

There was a long silence. Then, at last, 'Oh that.'

'Do you mean to say that Mrs Ross's daughter never left you and her children?—that she has been with you all the time and is still your wife?'

'Well, yes . . . but let me get Celia.'

'It is not necessary. She will hear from Mrs Ross's solicitor. There is enough money to cover the cremation and any other expenses. There is no need for me to speak to Celia,' and I rang off.

Afterwards I sat for a long time trying to reconcile myself to these new ideas. How like Aunt Louise, and how like her daughter. They had run circles round me. All my moilings and toilings over Aunt Louise!

During the next few weeks the thoughts continued to come and go. How much of the plan had Aunt Louise understood? Had even Mrs Girdlestone known about it? It might have been easy for Celia to persuade herself that it would all make little difference to me. Even if she could not have so persuaded herself *it would have made no difference*. Who should understand that better than I.

At least Celia's marriage seemed to have been saved. She could not have had an easy childhood. It would have been sad if her marriage, also, had been sacrificed.

One thing I could do, and I did it. I sent Celia a bill for everything, as far as I could remember, Aunt Louise had

[51]

This extract from a **dictionary** page is in complete contrast. Readers need access to individual chunks of information. Dictionary design has developed a grammar of signals to guide the reader around each entry. Dictionaries usually employ a shorthand repertory of conventions (because of the need to save space), so typographic variation is needed to reinforce differences and similarities between items that might otherwise be missed. Ambiguities are reduced wherever possible: different kinds of brackets and separating characters are used to surround different elements; labels and foreign words are set in distinctive type. Headwords (the words that are looked up) need to be immediately obvious, and are set in a heavier type, sometimes larger than text. They are made prominent by projecting further left than all other text.

A dictionary typeface is chosen to avoid ambiguities and reinforce differences. The best dictionary typefaces resemble newspaper typefaces in appearing larger than they really are, but the critical test is the balance between the plain, italic, and bold versions. The best heavy types are not those which achieve maximum blackness – these often look clogged, and word profiles suffer – but those which achieve maximum difference from the surrounding text. Typefaces which show more differences between individual characters are more successful than those where several letters of the alphabet can be confused because they share the same shapes.

A typeface consists of variant (but related) styles of alphabet. Using these different styles allows items to be emphasized.

---

accountable   7

take account of (or **take into account**) consider (*took their age into account*). turn to account (or **good account**) turn to one's advantage. [French: related to COUNT[1]]

accountable *adj.* **1** responsible; required to account for one's conduct. **2** explicable, understandable. □ **accountability** /-'bɪlɪtɪ/ *n.*

accountant *n.* professional keeper or verifier of accounts. □ **accountancy** *n.*

accounting *n.*

accoutrements /ə'ku:trəmənts/ *n.pl.* (*US* **accouterments** /-təmənts/) **1** equipment, trappings. **2** soldier's equipment excluding weapons and clothes. [French]

accredit /ə'kredɪt/ *v.* (-**t-**) **1** (foll. by *to*) attribute (a saying etc.) to. **2** (foll. by *with*) credit (a person) with (a saying etc.). **3** (usu. foll. by *to* or *at*) send (an ambassador etc.) with credentials. **4** gain influence for or make credible (an adviser, a statement, etc.). [French: related to CREDIT]

accredited *adj.* **1** officially recognized. **2** generally accepted.

accretion /ə'kri:ʃ(ə)n/ *n.* **1** growth or increase by accumulation, addition, or organic enlargement. **2** the resulting whole. **3 a** matter so added. **b** adhesion of this to the core matter. [Latin *cresco cret-* grow]

accrue /ə'kru:/ *v.* (-**ues, -ued, -uing**) (often foll. by *to*) come as a natural increase or advantage, esp. financial. [Latin: related to ACCRETION]

accumulate /ə'kju:mjʊ,leɪt/ *v.* (-**ting**) **1** acquire an increasing number or quantity of; amass, collect. **2** grow numerous; increase. [Latin: related to CUMULUS]

accumulation /ə,kju:mjʊ'leɪʃ(ə)n/ *n.* **1** accumulating, being accumulated. **2** accumulated mass. **3** growth of capital by continued interest. □ **accumulative** /ə'kju:mjʊlətɪv/ *adj.*

accumulator *n.* **1** rechargeable electric cell. **2** bet placed on a sequence of events, with the winnings and stake from each placed on the next.

accusative /ə'kju:zətɪv/ *Gram* expressing the object of an ac of or in this case.

accusatory /ə'kju:zətərɪ/ *ac* implying accusation.

accuse /ə'kju:z/ *v.* (-**sing**) (ofte *of*) charge with a fault or crim [Latin *accusare*: related to CAt

accustom /ə'kʌstəm/ *v.* (fol make used to (*accustomed hin ship*). [French: related to CUST

accustomed *adj.* **1** (usu. foll. b to. **2** customary, usual.

ace *n.* **1** playing-card etc. with spot and generally signifying person who excels in some a pilot who has shot down mar aircraft. **3** (in tennis) unr stroke (esp. a service). *adj. sl* lent. □ within an ace of on the [Latin *as* unity]

acellular /eɪ'seljʊlə(r)/ *adj.* h cells; not consisting of cells.

-aceous *suffix* forming adjecti sense 'of the nature of', es natural sciences (*herbaceous*)

acerbic /ə'sɜ:bɪk/ *adj.* harsh a esp. in speech or manner. □ **ac** (*pl.* **-ies**). [Latin *acerbus* sour]

acetaldehyde /æsɪ'tældɪ,haɪ ourless volatile liquid aldehy ACETIC, ALDEHYDE]

acetate /'æsɪ,teɪt/ *n.* **1** salt o acetic acid, esp. the cellulos fabric made from this.

acetic /ə'si:tɪk/ *adj.* of or like [Latin *acetum* vinegar]

acetic acid *n.* clear liquid ac vinegar its characteristic tast

acetone /'æsɪ,təʊn/ *n.* colour tile liquid that dissolves org pounds, esp. paints, varnishe

acetylene /ə'setɪ,li:n/ *n.* hyd gas burning with a bright fla esp. in welding.

ache /eɪk/ *n.* **1** continuous du mental distress. *v.* (-**ching**) su or be the source of an ache. lish]

achieve /ə'tʃi:v/ *v.* (-**ving**) **1**

headword
headword

Bembo bold (*top*) achieves maximum blackness by thickening up all parts of the letter and reducing the space inside each letter. Old Style bold (*bottom*) only thickens up the main parts of the letter, and retains maximum space inside each letter.

Conventions are not static. The Bible page shown here, which gives prominence to the 'literary' qualities of the text by infrequent paragraphing and the use of narrative headings, is typical of those produced over the past twenty years. A King James Bible will show a different emphasis, with each verse a separate paragraph, larger verse numbers, and no narrative headings.

In this **Bible** page there is an adherence to convention that is almost complete. The text is set in two columns, with large chapter numbers and division into verses indicated by smaller raised numbers. The text, although continuous, is not really intended for reading through from cover to cover: so the apparatus of book title and of verse and chapter numbers must be clear enough to provide access points for a reader seeking a particular passage. Convention is rooted in function, but reinforced by the status of the text: alternative presentations might not be immediately seen as Bibles.

If a convention works, use it.

THE LETTER OF PAUL TO THE
ROMANS

The gospel of Christ

1 FROM Paul, servant of Christ Jesus, called by God to be an apostle and set apart for the service of his gospel.
[2] This gospel God announced beforehand in sacred scriptures through his prophets. [3-4] It is about his Son: on the human level he was a descendant of David, but on the level of the spirit—the Holy Spirit—he was proclaimed Son of God by an act of power that raised him from the dead: it is about Jesus Christ our Lord. [5] Through him I received the privilege of an apostolic commission to bring people of all nations to faith and obedience in his name, [6] including you who have heard the call and belong to Jesus Christ.
[7] I send greetings to all of you in Rome,

power of God for everyone who has faith—the Jew first, but the Greek also—[17] because in it the righteousness of God is seen at work, beginning in faith and ending in faith; as scripture says, 'Whoever is justified through faith shall gain life.'

God's judgement on sin

[18] DIVINE retribution is to be seen at work, falling from heaven on all the impiety and wickedness of men and women who in their wickedness suppress the truth. [19] For all that can be known of God lies plain before their eyes; indeed God himself has disclosed it to them. [20] Ever since the world began his invisible attributes, that is to say his everlasting power and deity, have been visible to the eye of reason, in the things he has made.

The wedding invitation

Although this is a piece of important information, conventional wording and style are given prominence over legibility and economy. There have been severely beautiful modernist invitations, but nobody wants a dull one.

Typefaces can have style!

MR & MRS CYRIL HEAD

request the pleasure of the company of

at the marriage of their daughter

Donna Marie

to

Mr Adrian Chamberlain

at Christ Church, Reading on Saturday 10 September at 1 pm

and afterwards at The Mill House, Swallowfields

RSVP · 226 CULVER ROAD, READING, BERKSHIRE RG3 6AU

Note the sparing use of very ornate script initials in the example. Typefaces which imitate formal handwriting have been used for centuries. Their very style and formality makes them unsuitable for continuous text, and it is a mistake to use them for everyday correspondence, where plainer typefaces are needed.

What is typography?

The instruction manual

The page shown below aims to provide information. The key typographic feature is the reduction of the text to short paragraphs, breaking it down into understandable units. The writing and layout allow the reader to access the information in a variety of ways: it is possible to read through continuously, but the strong headings act as points where the reader can navigate around the text. Readers may choose to skip (if the text is irrelevant) or read on. Non-symbolic graphic devices (rules in this example; blobs are also used) reinforce this deliberate breaking up of the text.

Using the same typeface in different weights allows a unity to be imposed on a complex page.

Matching software to document preparation tasks
There are three different classes of desktop publishing software: word-processing, drawing, and page make-up software.

Word-processing software
mainly for originating text.

Should provide tools that help you work with text (such as routines to search the whole text for particular words or letter combinations and spelling checkers that allow you to create your own dictionaries of acceptable spellings).

Drawing software
for originating drawings, charts, and diagrams; can be good for tables.

Should include a wide range of tools for drawing different kinds of shapes, lines, and curves, and for moving them about on the page, either singly or as groups.

Page make-up software
for assembling the different elements of documents (text and illustrations) into pages.

Should take text and illustrations from word-processing and drawing software into different fields on the page (such as main and subsidiary columns); should allow fine adjustments to the typography of the text and the sizing and positioning of illustrations.

The distinctions between different kinds of software are not clear-cut: some word processors include simple drawing tools, or have formatting commands so you can produce multiple columns of text, as if you were using page make-up software; page make-up software also includes drawing tools and some text editing tools.

In developing typographic design skills, the first imperative is to see how others have done it and judge how successful they have been. The typographer's palette is the range of typefaces available, and the sizes and arrangements he can use them in. The succeeding chapters aim to provide technical information, but also give insights into why certain designs communicate effectively in particular circumstances.

The purpose of typographic design is constantly to renew the relationship between author, text, and reader. Informed experimentation with new and old typographic forms and genres, transposing, borrowing, overturning, is the way typography has always developed. Because we need to absorb increasingly complex information more quickly, and because there is more printed matter clamouring for our attention, it is important that clarity and the effective transmission of information are at the heart of all typographic design.

2

What is a typeface?

Before the advent of desktop publishing, only professional typesetting systems were able to set text in real typefaces to traditional standards. If you wanted to set your own type at home or at the office, typewriters, word-processor printers, or Letraset were the only available options. On typewriters and word-processor printers the range of typefaces and sizes was limited, and making changes to those available involved expensive hardware. Letraset rub-down lettering offered a large variety of styles, but was only practical for short texts in large sizes.

The democratization of type

Desktop publishing arrived in 1985 and transformed the world of text composition. In one important respect there was now no difference between professional typesetting systems and word processing: both were able to use the same typefaces, thanks to the emergence of a standard computer format for storing typefaces called PostScript. PostScript also allows type to be set at any size, whereas typewriters and word processors were restricted to a single size or small range of sizes.

Desktop systems are no longer tied to low-quality printers: a document using PostScript format typefaces can be printed out on low-resolution office printers or high-quality typesetting devices. The structure of the text – type sizes, line endings, page breaks, etc. – remains constant: only the sharpness of reproduction varies when a better-quality output system is chosen.

The importance of the device-independence of PostScript documents cannot be overemphasized, as it created a single market for typography. Designers and authors,

PostScript Helvetica
PostScript Times

Adobe, the software company that developed PostScript, made a licensing agreement with Linotype, one of the oldest manufacturers of traditional typesetting equipment. Helvetica and Times, based on designs owned by Linotype, were among the earliest Adobe PostScript typefaces, and are the most common in use. Typefaces licensed from ITC were added to create the 'Laser-Writer 35' (35 fonts, actually 10 typefaces).

who had hitherto been only the specifiers (or victims) of design, could now become implementers, controlling typeface, point size, indeed all the details of the typesetting. As with most revolutions, glorious benefits were promised and much chaos actually ensued. Early page make-up programs had few refinements, and many designers and authors underestimated the skill and craftsmanship that compositors, working in a rule-bound social environment with long-standing traditions, put into their work.

The situation has now stabilized: dtp applications have matured and genuinely offer many of the features of earlier professional typesetting systems. Whole sections of the publishing (and printing) industry have gone desktop. And, importantly, the range of typefaces in PostScript (and now TrueType) format has increased to a point where typography to professional standards can be undertaken using dtp technology.

PostScript and TrueType

PostScript is a page description language: a way of describing, in the form of a computer program, all the elements that make up a typeset page. Words, rules, boxes, tints, and illustrations can all be described in the PostScript language.

When you get your Macintosh or PC to print a page it prepares a PostScript program of the whole page, which the printer executes. This execution is the creation of a complete image of the page. The resolution of the image is dependent not on the incoming PostScript data, but on the capabilities of the output device: a LaserWriter using toner-and-plain-paper technology will produce a low-resolution image with 300 dots per inch; a Linotronic 330 using bromide or film technology will produce a high-resolution image with 2540 dots per inch.

A particular typeface can only be printed on a PostScript device if it is equipped with that typeface in PostScript format, or if the typeface is downloaded as part of the program.

TrueType (developed by Apple and Microsoft) is an alternative format for typefaces which works from the user's point of view in exactly the same way as the PostScript format. TrueType can be used with page description languages including PostScipt. At the time of writing there are far fewer typefaces available in TrueType format.

What is a typeface?

Some typefaces come built into every PostScript device. These are the 'LaserWriter 35'. Although they are there, they are not indispensable, and it can be argued that they do not represent a considered cross-section of typefaces that are available – especially for use at low resolution on a laser printer. You do not need to stay with these typefaces: PostScript typefaces can be bought from a variety of manufacturers. These include firms who have been manufacturers of machinery and typefaces for professional type-composition since the end of the nineteenth century, as well as newer suppliers who exploit the ease with which electronic typefaces can be created and distributed.

Times

Helvetica

New Century Schoolbook

Palatino

Courier

Zapf Chancery

Bookman

Avant Garde

The 'LaserWriter 35' sought to provide a range of typefaces for a variety of uses. The introduction of PostScript typefaces was an important and commendable move to replace the poorly drawn typefaces previously associated with computer display and print-outs. Computerized communication at last joined the mainstream of typography. But it is important to understand the limitations of the typefaces which make up the core set of fonts on LaserWriters.

Helvetica and Times were chosen because of their wide popularity among designers and printers. Both faces are very closely spaced, however, and can looked cramped at small sizes, especially at low resolution. Neither looks convincing when used for correspondence.

New Century Schoolbook was a good choice of general-purpose typeface, and Palatino provided a bookish typeface. Palatino has an italic which is fussy at small sizes, especially at low resolution.

Courier provided a 'typewriter lookalike' typeface, but it is anaemic and not as widely useful as a typewriter face should be. Zapf Chancery, an 'artistic' script, is best avoided altogether: it is too wide to be elegant at large sizes, and is unreadable when used for text.

Bookman and Avant Garde were fashionable advertising typefaces in the 1970s, with characteristic close spacing and enormous x-heights. They now look dated for display, and are uncomfortable to read when used for continuous text.

To avoid your work looking 'desktop published', it is best to restrict your use of these typefaces and consider the wider range of typefaces from both traditional and new typeface manufacturers that are now available in PostScript. The typeface examples in the second part of this book will help you make informed choices.

Typefaces and fonts

These terms need to be distinguished to avoid confusion. A *typeface* is a family of alphabets related by design and produced by a single manufacturer.

Each typeface family consists of variant *fonts*, usually roman, italic, and bold; sometimes bold italic, and sometimes other condensed and expanded, lighter and heavier variants. (For a fuller explanation of these terms see pp. 40–3.) Several manufacturers may make versions of the same typeface, different in design details. Each font contains a collection of characters, known as the *character set* for that font. In PostScript and TrueType this is theoretically standardized, but in fact some fonts have a limited character set (capitals only, for instance) or an extended or altered character set which includes ornamental or alternative characters.

Three typeface families

Traditional book typefaces such as Bembo have only recently been equipped with more than one bold weight.

Univers was planned from the outset to be a family with a variety of light, bold, condensed, and expanded forms. Variations were planned to be logical , and the use of a numbering system to classify the weights emphasizes the 'rational' nature of the design.

The Gill Sans family has grown more erratically, and letter forms show less uniformity of design from weight to weight (compare the various shapes of lower case a and capital S). There are no italic forms of the two boldest weights.

Bembo roman	Univers 45	Univers 47	Gill Sans light
Bembo italic	*Univers 45*	*Univers 47*	*Gill Sans light italic*
Bembo small caps	Univers 55	Univers 57	Gill Sans
Bembo semi bold	*Univers 55*	*Univers 57*	*Gill Sans italic*
Bembo semi bold italic	**Univers 65**	**Univers 67**	**Gill Sans bold**
Bembo bold	***Univers 65***	***Univers 67***	***Gill Sans bold italic***
Bembo bold italic	**Univers 75**		**Gill Sans bold condensed**
Bembo extra bold	***Univers 75***		**Gill Sans extra bold**
Bembo extra bold italic			**Gill Sans ultra bold**

abcdefghijklmnopqrstuvwxyz
ABCDEFGHIJKLMNOPQRSTUVWXYZ
0123456789
, . ; : ' " " ' „ · « » ? ¿ ! i ( ) [ ] / | - – — …
* § † ¶ & % ‰ £ $ ¥ ƒ ° •
fi fl æ Æ œ Œ ı ß ª º
å Å Â ä Ä á Á à À ç Ç Î ï Ï í Í ì Ì Ê ë Ë é É è È Ô ö
Ö ó Ó ò Ò ø Ø Û ü Ü ú Ú ù Ù Ÿ
@ # ® © ™ \ ^ ~ ˘ < > { } ¤ ' "
+ = ± ≈ ∞ ≠ ≤ ≥ π ∂ ∫ √ ∑ ≈ Ω ÷

This chart shows the characters that can be accessed from a Macintosh keyboard in a PostScript font. Accented characters are created by the dtp software, which combines accent and character from the font as required. There are further characters which exist in the full PostScript character set (see p. 18) but cannot be accessed from the Macintosh keyboard in its English-language version.

Special fonts

There are also special fonts known as *expert sets* or *expert collections*, which, instead of normal upper and lower case letters, contain small capitals, alternative figures, decorative swash letters, ligatures (tied letters), superiors (small raised figures), and ornaments such as flowers and flourishes.

Fonts such as Symbol, Zapf Dingbats, and Universal Pi are not strictly speaking members of any typeface family, but collections of symbols which can be used with a variety of typefaces.

The Symbol font is intended to be a 'neutral' collection of characters that will work with any typeface: it works best with Times.

ABCDEFGHIJKLMNOPQRSTUVWXYZ
1234567890 fffiflffffiffl ¼½⅛⅜ 1

This expert set (for Monotype Ehrhardt) contains small capitals, alternative figures, and ligatures (letters which are joined together to make certain combinations appear tidier). Ligatures fi and fl are also in the normal PostScript character set.

ABCDEFGHIJKLMNOPQRSTUVWXYZ

This expert collection (for Adobe Garamond) contains special fancy alternative capitals, known as swash letters.

This chart shows all the characters that form a standard PostScript font. It differs from the chart of characters which can be accessed from the Macintosh keyboard, which includes combinations of accents and characters.

Letters, numbers, punctuation, and accents will be specially drawn for each font as part of the design of the typeface. These characters must obviously share common features. Some characters are considered less demanding: mathematical and commercial signs are often not redrawn for a typeface, but pulled 'off the shelf'. The mathematical characters which are part of many typefaces are in fact taken from the Adobe Symbol font.

The grid system in the chart identifies the hexadecimal number of each character, the standard numerical value by which computers identify characters. The small numbers below each character show its width in *units of set* (see p. 51).

	0 (0)	1 (16)	2 (32)	3 (48)	4 (64)	5 (80)	6 (96)	7 (112)	8 (128)	9 (144)	A (160)	B (176)	C (192)	D (208)	E (224)	F (240)
0 (0)	NUL	DLE	SP 250	0 500	@ 765	P 549	' 235	p 507	250	250	250	250	250	— 1000	250	250
1 (1)	SOH	DC1	! 220	1 500	A 623	Q 795	a 404	q 497	250	250	¡ 220	– 500	` 360	250	Æ 850	æ 585
2 (2)	STX	DC2	" 404	2 500	B 605	R 645	b 500	r 332	250	250	¢ 500	† 480	´ 360	250	250	250
3 (3)	ETX/Enter	DC3	# 500	3 500	C 696	S 489	c 400	s 323	250	250	£ 500	‡ 480	^ 360	250	ª 332	250
4 (4)	EOT	DC4	$ 500	4 500	D 780	T 660	d 509	t 307	250	250	/ 100	· 250	˘ 360	250	250	250
5 (5)	ENQ	NAK	% 844	5 500	E 584	U 746	e 396	u 512	250	250	¥ 500	250	¯ 360	250	250	¹ 257
6 (6)	ACK	SYN	& 818	6 500	F 538	V 676	f 290	v 432	250	250	ƒ 500	¶ 500	˘ 360	250	250	250
7 (7)	BEL	ETB	' 235	7 500	G 747	W 960	g 446	w 660	250	250	§ 506	• 388	˙ 360	250	250	250
8 (8)	BS	CAN	(320	8 500	H 806	X 643	h 515	x 432	250	250	¤ 500	‚ 215	¨ 360	250	Ł 559	ł 261
9 (9)	HT	EM	) 320	9 500	I 338	Y 574	i 257	y 438	250	250	' 235	„ 384	250	250	Ø 795	ø 486
A (10)	LF	SUB	* 394	: 250	J 345	Z 641	j 253	z 377	250	250	" 404	" 404	° 360	250	Œ 1012	œ 729
B (11)	VT	ESC/Clear	+ 500	; 250	K 675	[320	k 482	{ 320	250	250	« 378	» 378	¸ 360	250	º 387	ß 523
C (12)	FF	FS	, 250	< 500	L 553	\ 309	l 247	| 239	250	250	‹ 233	… 1000	250	250	250	250
D (13)	CR	GS	- 320	= 500	M 912	] 320	m 787	} 320	250	250	› 233	‰ 1144	˝ 360	250	250	250
E (14)	SO	RS	. 250	> 500	N 783	^ 500	n 525	~ 500	250	250	fi 522	250	˛ 360	250	250	250
F (15)	SI	US	/ 327	? 321	O 795	_ 500	o 486	DEL 250	250	250	fl 522	¿ 321	ˇ 360	250	250	250

LaserQuill—Windsor

18

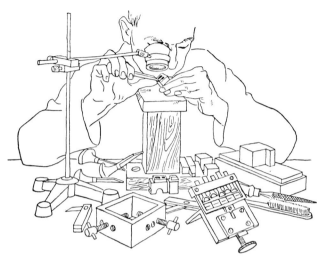

Creating type directly from drawings is relatively new in the history of typography. Until the middle of the nineteenth century all designs were literally cut in metal at the size they would be reproduced. The model letter thus produced (the punch) was sunk into a metal blank to produce a mould (the matrix), from which type could subsequently be cast.

How are typefaces created and stored?

The typeface drawing programs that are available for personal computers allow you to draw outlines directly on screen; but most professional type design by the major manufacturers relies on hand-drawn pencil originals, which have to be *digitized* – i.e. read electronically and stored in a computer. Points along the outside of each letter are selected, and the paths between these points are described mathematically. Letters are therefore stored as mathematical descriptions of their outlines (hence the term *outline font*).

An outline font description of a character can be mathematically transformed to produce sloped or condensed variants, rotated, mirror-imaged, and scaled to any size. The limits of these transformations and scalings are determined by the dtp program that you use.

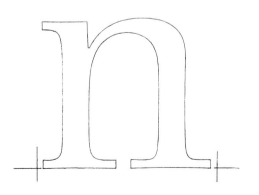

Drawing letters by hand is not an anachronism. Although regularity is a prime requirement of a successful typeface, absolute uniformity of elements is not. The serifs on opposite sides of a letter, for example, are often not exact mirror images of each other.

There is a strong argument for introducing controlled irregularities into a typeface to prevent a stultifying dullness pervading the design. The brain demands a level of variation in what the eye scans to remain alert. It may be this monotony of form that makes over-regularized sans serifs (see p. 31) tiring to read: they are simply not interesting enough.

When the character has to be printed, the outline serves as a template for the creation of the character by the output device. All PostScript output devices, e.g. laser printers, are *raster* devices – that is, they build up the total page image strip by strip, like a television picture. A scanning electron beam either exposes photosensitive material which passes beneath it (for imagesetters), or energizes a drum so that toner powder is attracted to the charge (for laser printers). The number of times the beam can be switched on and off during its scan is usually related to its thickness and the advance of the material that will receive the image, so the image will be laid down on a grid with a certain number of *dots per inch*.

The program that controls the beam to generate the strips from the outline data is called the rasterizer. The creation of the whole image is called *raster image processing* (abbreviated as 'rip', hence the verb 'to rip' meaning to print out, usually at high resolution).

At low resolution the grid of dots available to create the image will be coarse, and allow a very imperfect rendering of the refined outline shape. Curves are seen as steps, and the white spaces within letters may fill in. The coarseness can be improved by *hints*: the rasterizer adjusts the outline relative to the available grid, which ensures that certain features are regularized and others are not lost completely. Hints therefore allow characters to retain recognizable and regular features, but at the expense of some distortion of the letter forms. This distortion, however, is less than that caused by unhinted rasterization, when two normally equal parts of a letter may print at different thicknesses, or individual letters appear to jump up and down instead of aligning regularly.

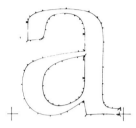

Character drawing with digitization points added. Only the outline will be stored: the character will be filled on output by the rasterizer.

A very low resolution (72 dpi) image of a character compared with the original outline, showing how it is built up on a grid of square dots. 72 dpi is the resolution of a computer screen.

Enlargement of a character produced by a low-resolution laser printer.

Enlargement of a character produced by a high-resolution imagesetter.

At higher resolution, the laser beam will be thinner, and the material will advance in smaller increments, so that the available grid of dots is much finer. Hints become less necessary and character shapes can be imaged very accurately. In practical terms there are three print resolutions worth understanding:

300 dots per inch (dpi) is the resolution of laser printers. It is sufficient for proofing, or for final output if hinted fonts are used and higher-resolution output is uneconomical. Tints (shades of grey) and halftones (photographs) cannot be rendered with any accuracy: they will look coarse and 'desktop published'.

1270 dpi is the lowest resolution of professional imagesetters, such as the Monotype Prism and Linotronic 200. It will give perfectly accurate type, but halftones and fine tints do not reproduce well.

2540 upwards. This is the resolution of the highest-quality imagesetters, such as the Linotronic 330. It is capable of outputting the finest tints and halftones. You need this quality of resolution to output a photograph.

A schematic diagram of one sweep of the raster, or pattern of strips, that makes up the total image. The material receiving the image advances by the thickness of the beam to receive the next sweep. Video screen displays are also built up this way.

<u>Underscore</u>
Outline
Shadow

Outline shadow

As well as offering the ability to scale a font to any size or to rotate or change the relative width of a letter, PostScript offers some standard variations which are sometimes mistaken for specially drawn variant fonts, as they are displayed in menus alongside true variant fonts such as italic and bold. These are all electronic distortions of the basic font, and lack the optical corrections that a type designer brings to the task of producing variants from a basic design. They can look crude and obvious, and are best avoided.

Underscore is a particularly unsatisfactory method of emphasizing words in text. Derived from the limitations of the typewriter, where the basic typeface could only be modified, not changed, underscore should not be used when italic or bold fonts offer better contrast or emphasis.

By changing the German word <u>Herr</u> to <u>Narr</u>, the passage was perverted from 'he shall be thy <u>lord</u>' to 'he shall be thy <u>fool</u>'.

By changing the German word *Herr* to *Narr*, the passage was perverted from 'he shall be thy *lord*' to 'he shall be thy *fool*'.

ABCD
RSTU
abcdfg

The idea that a single design should be available in a range of sizes dates from the nineteenth century, when the development of the pantograph (a machine for copying an original at different sizes) made it possible to engrave matrices for several sizes from one original pattern. Before

ABCDE
RSTUV
abcdefg

then designs were cut size by size. The typeface we call Caslon, in its original metal version, is the range of types cut by the eighteenth-century typefounder William Caslon over a period of years (and includes one size he bought from another punch-cutter). Compare the two sizes above.

quickly

quickly

quickly

(*From top*) 6 pt, 8 pt, and 12 pt Monotype Bembo enlarged to show design differences due to optical scaling. (For further discussion of this typeface, see p. 110.)

Optical scaling

As well as the general characteristics of a new typeface, designer and manufacturer need to decide what range of sizes the typeface is most likely to be set in. This can be simplified to a distinction between small composition sizes (for newspaper classified advertisements, for example); text composition sizes (8 pt to 14 pt covers newspaper, book, and advertisement text); and display (conventionally sizes above 14 pt, used to set individual words and headlines rather than continuous text).

When each size of metal type was cut by hand, punch-cutters adjusted their designs size by size for both practical and aesthetic reasons. Smaller sizes had to be open and sturdy both to facilitate the cutting and casting process, and to give the maximum appearing size for readability. Larger sizes could have letters that fitted together more closely with finer strokes and detailing. This tradition of optical scaling was carried through into machine composition, and the Monotype cutting of Bembo shows how extreme variations can be played on the design of a type to maximize its effectiveness at each size.

Optical scaling was lost with the introduction of photo-mechanical typesetting, since all available sizes could be produced by the lens systems from a single master alphabet. Responsible manufacturers did make two or three variant 'sizes' of each typeface to work over restricted enlargement ranges, but it was extremely rare for a printer to install more than one version. This situation has remained the same, unfortunately, with digital typefaces. To restore a form of optical scaling, designers can resort to tinkering, such as increasing the space between letters and expanding the character shapes in small

What is a typeface?

Digital type at high resolution has banished the fuzzy edges from type. Font formats which use mathematical descriptions of curves have rescued letter forms from straight line segments.

6/8 pt

Digital type at high resolution has banished the fuzzy edges from type. Font formats which use mathematical descriptions of curves have rescued letter forms from straight line segments. We are promised non-linear scaling, to adjust the relative proportions of x-height to ascenders and descenders, and thick to thin stroke ratios.

6/8 pt

Digital type at high resolution has banished the fuzzy edges from type. Font formats which use mathematical descriptions of curves have rescued letter forms from straight line segments. We are promised non-linear scaling, to adjust the relative proportions of x-height to ascenders and descenders, and thick to thin stroke ratios.

6/8 pt

Digital type at high resolution has banished the fuzzy edges from type.

12/15 pt

Digital type at high resolution has banished the fuzzy edges from type. We are promised non-linear scaling.

12/15 pt

Digital type at high resolution has banished the fuzzy edges from type. We are promised non-linear scaling.

12/15 pt

Digital type

24/28 pt

Maximus, a typeface designed for small text composition.

Digital type at high resolution

24/28 pt

Joanna, a typeface designed for normal text composition.

Digital type at high resolution

24/28 pt

Helvetica compressed, a typeface designed for display use.

sizes, reducing space and condensing characters in large sizes. This needs time for experimentation and leads to a complex set of adjustments which have to be recalled and implemented for each change of size. A more reliable solution is to bypass the question by selecting different typefaces (or variations of a typeface) for use at different sizes, so that each typeface is chosen to perform best at the size at which it is used.

HSHS

HH

In artificially condensed type, vertical strokes lose weight and horizontal strokes appear to thicken.

HSHS

HH

In artificially expanded type, vertical strokes gain weight and horizontal strokes appear to lose weight.

In both cases, curves and diagonal strokes are violently distorted.

Manipulating fonts

An outline font can be manipulated to produce condensed and expanded versions. The versions are simply mathematical transformations, and do not include the optical correction required to produce true variants.

This can easily produce visual inconsistencies if extreme values of condensing and expansion are used: as a rule, 5 per cent is about the most that a typeface will tolerate before the distortion begins to become painful. Sans serif typefaces are generally more tolerant of such adjustment than typefaces with serifs.

There are alternatives to this simple electronic distortion. A more subtle kind of transformation can be performed if PostScript Multiple Master typefaces are available. Instead of generating bitmaps from a single outline font, this system produces characters derived from information in four or more outline fonts. Thus an intermediate stage between a roman and a bold font can be generated, and between a normal width and a condensed font. The fonts used as starting points for the interpolation of variants need to be specially encoded. A technique similar to this (the Ikarus system) has been used by type manufacturers for several years to produce intermediate weights of typefaces automatically.

There are two benefits of the Multiple Master approach to variant fonts: the condensed and expanded versions produced do not suffer from the optical distortions of transformations from a single font; and variant weights as well as widths can be interpolated, for example to produce a heavier weight more suitable for reversing white out of black, or for video screen display.

Interpolation
Interpolation
Interpolation

This example of interpolating was done on the professional Ikarus M system. The middle line was interpolated from the ones above and below, but was deliberately programmed to be more similar to the bold than to the roman font.

The drawback of the technique is that the digitization points of the two or more master fonts must be exactly compatible: this rules out (or at least makes very difficult) interpolating between fonts with different design characteristics, and may lead to an undesirable reduction in the individuality of the extreme weights from which others are derived.

gg aa

Designing a bold font does not consist of simply thickening up the stroke weights. Bembo (*left*) and Helvetica show how the shapes of letters have to be altered as well. This feature makes interpolating between such fonts, to produce an intermediate variant, an extremely complex procedure.

A Multiple Masters typeface consists of master designs, shown here at the four corners of a matrix of possible variants that can be produced from them.

Manipulating the character set

We have seen above how the character set (the collection of characters that each font contains) is set by the font manufacturer. This usually relates to the published standards for PostScript and TrueType. But there is no standardized character set, or allocation of characters to the keyboard, for Greek, Russian, phonetic, or other special fonts. It is possible to reallocate the existing characters within a font with tools such as Font Mixer. If you wished, you could create a hybrid font with, say, certain Greek characters or frequently used special symbol characters replacing ones you do not normally use.

Wayland's Smithy ☞ WHITE HORSE

To avoid font changes the fist character (from Universal News with Commercial Pi) can be incorporated into a Swift font using Font Mixer.

Design quality and type manufacturers

The rapid increase in the number of typefaces available is a relatively recent phenomenon: traditionally printers held the minimum number of typefaces in the minimum number of sizes, as each addition represented significant capital investment. In the days before photocomposition the sheer bulk and weight of metal type, too, was an important factor. Type manufacturers, both foundries and composing machine manufacturers, produced new designs on a regular basis. In the twentieth century foundries tended to be innovative in releasing new typefaces for advertising and display work, while Linotype and Monotype concentrated on newspaper and book faces respectively.

The first four decades of this century saw the most remarkable development of new typefaces from these manufacturers – designs based on historical examples and completely new typefaces suitable for developments in printing technology. Because of the long experience of both the foundries and composing machine manufacturers, all of these typefaces were technically sound and many were exceedingly beautiful. Printers selecting from such ranges could not fail to install reasonably well-designed typefaces.

The widespread introduction of photocomposition in the 1960s (machines had appeared as early as the 1930s) changed this completely. New manufacturers sprang up, without the typographic resources of the traditional manufacturers, and offered typefaces which were at best plagiarisms, at worst travesties, of existing designs. Typefaces available on the early Compugraphic machines were particularly unpleasant, but the machines were cheap and reliable, and sold well. Even experienced manufacturers often failed to make the necessary adjustments to their existing typefaces so as to render them suitable for photocomposition, with too many anaemic and loosely fitted designs. There is still too little compensation for the thinning down of typefaces that high-resolution output and printing on glossy paper produce. This is most noticeable in the traditional seriffed book faces. They can often look unhappily flimsy when printed from digital output by lithography. The original metal type was designed so that the spread of ink under pressure would thicken up the stroke weights. Lithographic printing techniques do not add this thickening; indeed, sometimes the characters are actually eroded. Weak letter forms result when the digital version does not compensate for this thickening, known as 'ink squash' or 'ink spread'.

The current transformation in design quality of typefaces stems directly from the change from photomechanical to digital technology in composition. This eliminated the blurring of characters which was inevitable with systems that drew letters on cathode ray tubes and projected them through lens systems, and enabled the move away from typeface storage formats that were specific to particular manufacturers. Any typeface in a digital format such as PostScript and TrueType can be output on any composition machine equipped with a compatible page description language. The sudden availability of cheaper typeface digitization software made typeface production a practical rather than a theoretical proposition for many designers, and a plethora of small 'foundries' sprang up.

Agfa (who succeeded Compugraphic, and have raised their standards since photomechanical days), Bitstream, Linotype, and Monotype issued large numbers of typefaces, including versions of famous metal designs. Design companies such as the Font Bureau issued revivals of historical curiosities. Émigré Graphics specialized in new typefaces that relished looking like bitmaps; and exciting new typefaces such as Scala and Officina emerged from The Netherlands and Germany.

The larger companies do not release typefaces that are not reasonably well drawn and well digitized, although all produce some typefaces which are fashionable rather than useful. Smaller suppliers may be able to supply a typeface which the major companies have not got round to yet. And because the appearance and detail of a typeface are so important, you may simply prefer x's Baskerville to y's. The only caveat is to avoid suppliers of '100 PostScript faces for $99' – you are unlikely to find anything usable in such collections of 1960s photolettering rejects.

The notes on the following pages describe manufacturers whose typefaces are discussed in this book: they should be read in conjunction with the further details and addresses on pp. 124–6.

What is a typeface?

Adobe

Lucida Lucida Sans
Lucida *Lucida Sans*
Lucida **Lucida Sans**
Lucida ***Lucida Sans***

Adobe started desktop publishing, and its typefaces are the 'LaserWriter 35' on every PostScript device. These include less than ideal versions (redrawn from the much better Linotype and ITC originals) of Times, Helvetica, Baskerville, and Century Schoolbook. Adobe then launched an original type design programme, which has resulted in such useful typefaces as the Lucida and Minion families, and revivals such as Adobe Garamond. Minion, with its separate text and display versions, swash (fancy) capitals, small capitals, and titling (large display) capitals, shows how complex a typeface family can be.

Agfa

Rotis Semisans Rotis SemiSerif
Rotis Semisans **Rotis SemiSerif**
Rotis Sans Serif Rotis Serif
Rotis Sans Serif *Rotis Serif*

As with Bitstream, the Agfa range lacks the backlist that Monotype and Linotype enjoy, and for many years it concentrated on clones or licensed versions of those manufacturers' typefaces. Its best efforts are now in developing interesting display rather than text typefaces.

Bitstream

Bitstream Charter
Bitstream Charter
Bitstream Charter
Bitstream Charter
Bitstream Charter
Bitstream Charter

Founded by staff who left the US Linotype operations, Bitstream started as a type design and digitization company rather than a manufacturer of equipment. This strong design base ensures that the interpretation of typefaces is aesthetically and technically excellent. Bitstream Galliard is the most pleasing version of the typeface; Bitstream Charter is an excellent typeface for low-resolution output.

Many of its typefaces are reworkings of designs originated by earlier manufacturers. Bitstream uses two
names for these typefaces, its own and a 'Bitstream version of' name, e.g. Dutch 811, Bitstream version of
Olympian.

ITC

The International Typeface Corporation commissions
designs but does not sell typefaces to end users.
Foundries are licensed to manufacture and distribute
the designs. In the 1970s ITC concentrated on typefaces
for the New York advertising market. Early designs such
as Avant Garde and Benguiat seemed dynamic at the
time, but the relentless issuing of over-regularized, large
x-height faces, each in a huge range of weights, soon
began to pall. ITC Officina may herald a change of direc-
tion: a genuinely useful typeface with both seriffed and
sans serif variants, it is excellent for informal and correspondence use. ITC Mendoza is in the idiom of Palatino,
providing a welcome alternative, especially for informal
use.

ITC Officina Sans
ITC Officina Sans
ITC Officina Sans
ITC Officina Sans
ITC Officina Serif
ITC Officina Serif
ITC Officina Serif
ITC Officina Serif

Linotype

Founded in 1886, this is the best type library for newspaper and sans serif display types (Olympian, Excelsior;
Neue Helvetica, Univers, Frutiger). Some excellent faces
(e.g. Janson Text) are very closely fitted. Linotype logically
calls fonts which contain small capitals 'small capital
fonts' rather than expert sets or collections. These exist
for a range of classic book faces. Linotype continues its
programme of developing original typefaces, such as
Linotype Centennial and Avenir.

Univers   Olympian
Univers   *Olympian*
Univers   **Olympian**
Univers   ***Olympian***
Univers
Univers
Univers
Univers

Monotype

Founded in 1897, Monotype offers the best type library for traditional book composition typefaces, including Baskerville, Bembo, Garamond, Centaur, Times New Roman, all of which are equipped with expert sets to provide small capitals and old-style figures (see p. 42).

There are fewer original sans serif and display faces than Linotype offers. Some roman seriffed faces can be lighter than their metal forebears, although Monotype has carefully respaced many of its typefaces for PostScript format, tightening up designs that were previously too loose. This has the advantage of making them appear slightly darker in text setting. Like Linotype and Bitstream, Monotype has a programme of issuing new faces suitable for professional and dtp use, such as Calisto and Amasis.

Bembo
Bembo
Bembo
Bembo
Bembo
Bembo
Bembo
Bembo
BEMBO

Amasis
Amasis
Amasis
Amasis

Calisto
Calisto
Calisto
Calisto

3

How do typefaces differ?

Desktop publishing opens up an enormous range of typefaces to the non-expert user, and it is easy to be overwhelmed by the sheer number and think that differences between them, other than the most obvious, are insignificant or unimportant. This chapter offers two ways of recognizing the differences between typefaces – structural and historical.

It is worth remembering why there are so many typefaces. Those currently available represent a slice through typographic history, because each period has imposed its own style on type design and the best (or most memorable) have endured. They also represent responses to the vast range of printed matter that is produced, because typefaces are never designed in a vacuum: the best are responses to a particular design or production problem.

Seriffed and sans serif typefaces

The most obvious feature dividing typefaces, even to the inexperienced eye, is that some have small terminals (*serifs*) at the end of main strokes and some do not. These are called *seriffed* and *sans serif* typefaces. Serifs are regularizations of the finishing strokes found in Roman inscriptional lettering; these in turn represent the flick of the brush stroke that painted the letter on stone before it was incised. As well as the decorative purpose of finishing the main strokes of letters, serifs have the effect of providing horizontal flow between letters, emphasizing the line of reading, and helping individual characters combine into the word profiles which are so important for reading.

seriffed
sans serif

stressed
monoline

Most seriffed typefaces have strokes with clearly different thicknesses: they are described as having *stress*. Most sans serif typefaces have only a single apparent weight of stroke, and are said to be *monoline.*

Seriffed typefaces have always been the only ones considered for serious book or newspaper typography, where a large amount of continuous text is presented in small sizes of type. But sans serif faces are ideal for instant recognition of individual letters, and produce extremely legible word shapes for road signs, for example. Sans serifs can be used effectively for text composition if line length is kept short and space between lines is generous. A seriffed typeface will be easier for the reader if these conditions cannot be met.

CASLON'S
EGYPTIAN

Sans serifs are popularly considered a modern invention, but in fact inscriptional letter forms which have no serifs can be found dating from the fifteenth century, and the earliest metal type (confusingly called Caslon's Egyptian) dates from 1816.

Just as different typographic forms have associations with quality or authority, so different typefaces are assumed to have different 'atmosphere values'. The most common assumption is that seriffed typefaces are literary while sans serifs have a scientific or technical feel. This is partly true, but looking at scientific textbooks shows that hardly any use sans serif for continuous reading. The value of sans serif designs for complex typography comes from the ease with which variant weights and widths can be produced from the basic typeface without destroying its essential characteristics: this both provides a wide range of related but differentiated variants to be used together in a job, and makes available fonts which can be used in contrast to seriffed typefaces for headings, notes, captions, etc.

32

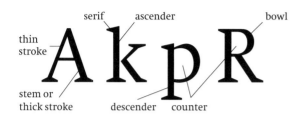

serif · ascender · bowl

thin stroke

stem or thick stroke · descender · counter

ascender line
x-height

baseline
descender line

serifs

horizontal
hairline
no bracket

oblique
blunt
with bracket

horizontal
hairline
with bracket

oblique
sharp
with bracket

horizontal
slab
no bracket

Categorizing by appearance

Deciding how to group and identify typefaces by appearance requires an analysis of the design features of individual letters and overall design characteristics of the alphabet.

The table overleaf will enable the user to consider the actual appearance of typefaces, rather than be misled by names. There is a long history of typefaces receiving evocative but misleading historical names: for example, none of the Garamonds available in PostScript format is directly based on types cut by the famous French punch-cutter Claude Garamond; and the Renaissance Cardinal Bembo did not design the typeface that bears his name (it is based on the types in which a book of his was printed).

When manufacturers use the same name for their typefaces, the inexperienced user will assume that the typefaces will look the same when typeset. Unfortunately this is not the case. Even where the International Typeface Corporation (ITC) commissions a typeface from a designer, and then supplies drawings to several manufacturers, differences may be significant. There is no guarantee that one manufacturer's type will bear more than a general resemblance to another's of the same name. The differences will often be in the critical areas of x-height, width, and weight, which actually affect appearing size and therefore legibility at a given point size.

How do typefaces differ?

	Seriffed typefaces		Sans serif typefaces	
angle of shading	oblique O Bembo	vertical o Bodoni	oblique e Clearface Gothic	vertical O Univers
contrast of thick and thin strokes	little contrast m Glypha	much contrast m Scotch Roman	no contrast o Futura	some contrast O Optima
x-height	large a Nimrod	small a Perpetua	large h Grotesque 37	small h Akzidenz
weight	heavy O Plantin	light O Garamond	very heavy a Antique Olive Nord	very light i Gill Light
width of letters	wide a Plantin	narrow a Joanna italic	wide g Franklin Gothic	narrow g Gill

Historical descriptions

Type historians divide typefaces into categories which relate to the main periods in the development of type design over the past five centuries. They are shown in the charts overleaf. These are the categories being referred to when you hear typefaces described as 'Old Face', 'Transitional', or 'a Geometrical sans serif'. These terms are valid for metal types, but are difficult to apply to some typefaces currently available, which may be hybrids combining features from several historical categories.

Certain details of letter form are associated with particular historical categories. The b without foot serif is characteristically Old Face; spurs developed in Transitional typefaces, growing into full-scale foot serifs in Modern faces. The tails of R are straight in Old Face, develop curves in the Transitional faces, and become distinctly curly in Modern faces.

Another characteristic development can be seen in the terminal of g and f. These develop from blunt pen stroke to become engraved, 'pot-hook' forms.

bgRf

Old Face · Monotype Bembo

bgRf

Transitional · Monotype Bell

bgRf

Modern · Monotype Scotch Roman

Seriffed typeface categories

Until the nineteenth century the book was the dominant typographic form, so the first three categories shown here are all styles for book composition.

Old Face designs originate from pen-drawn scripts, and show the influence of the broad, oblique nib.

Old Face designs from the late fifteenth century have oblique stress, where the thickest parts of the letters o and e are at the top right and bottom left. There is little contrast between thick and thin strokes, and serifs are oblique and bracketed.

From the mid-eighteenth century the *Transitional* faces were influenced by the calligraphy produced by the flexible steel nib. An intermediate stage between Old Face and Modern, these show a change towards vertical stress, where the thickest parts of the letters o and e are at the left and right.

From the late eighteenth century the *Modern* face developed, influenced by engraved letter forms and often taken to dazzling extremes. These show absolutely vertical stress, strong contrast between thick and thin strokes, horizontal, unbracketed serifs.

Bembo Monotype
Old Face

Baskerville Monotype
Transitional

Bodoni Linotype
Modern

Bodoni Linotype
Fat Face

Glypha Linotype
Egyptian

36

Sans serif typeface categories

Equivalent historical categories can be defined for sans serif typefaces.

Industrial Grotesque. The earliest sans serif forms, dating from the early nineteenth century, the most anonymous of all sans serifs.

Humanist sans serif (early twentieth century). With capitals based on classical Roman inscriptions, these are clearly traditional letter forms with the serifs removed.

Geometrical sans serif (early twentieth century). Based on 'ruler and compass' construction, and without apparent thick and thin stokes.

Regularized Industrial Grotesque. This group includes Helvetica, the most widely used sans serif typeface. Based on nineteenth-century designs, but considerably tidied up, often with an extensive range of weights and widths.

Grotesque 37 Font Bureau

19th-century Industrial Grotesque

Franklin Gothic Linotype

The Grotesque is called *Gothic* in the US

Gill Sans Monotype

20th-century Humanist sans serif

Futura Linotype

20th-century Geometrical sans serif

Univers Linotype

20th-century regularized Industrial Grotesque

Misleading names

In spite of its name, Monotype Garamond is based on sixteenth-century types by Jean Jannon and Robert Granjon. Confusingly, the most accurate revival of a type by Claude Garamond is probably Bitstream's Granjon, based on George W. Jones's Linotype face of the 1930s.

Bodoni, Baskerville, and Plantin were all immensely influential printers, and most of the typefaces bearing their names are tributes to their influence rather than the types they used. Modern Bodonis, for example, have been described as representing Bodoni at neither his best nor his worst, 'but certainly at his utmost'.

Monotype Garamond
Stempel Garamond
ITC Garamond Light

aaa
Monotype   Linotype   ITC

Garamond shows an extreme example, where typefaces suited to quite different purposes share the same name: Monotype Garamond is a finely drawn, accurate revival of a sixteenth-century typeface, suitable for refined bookwork; Linotype Stempel Garamond is a more robust typeface with a wider general application; and ITC Garamond Light is an advertising face with an enormous x-height and a wide variety of variants, not at all suited to text composition.

When Birmingham, for riots and for crimes,
Shall meet the keen reproach of future times,
Then shall she find, amongst our honoured race,
One name to save her from entire disgrace.

When Birmingham, for riots and for crimes,
Shall meet the keen reproach of future times,
Then shall she find, amongst our honoured race,
One name to save her from entire disgrace.

Baskerville shows two different interpretations of the eighteenth-century types of John Baskerville: both are equally removed from the original, but the Monotype version (*upper*) is austere and impassive while the ITC version (*lower*) has stronger colour contrast and a more lively feel (but unhappily short ascenders).

How do typefaces differ?

Adobe Times

The success of any process of design depends upon a sympathetic attitude on the part of the designer towards the material he undertakes to shape. The material, when its conditions are understood and met, itself meets the designer halfway. (8/9.5pt)

The success of any process of design depends upon a sympathetic attitude on the part of the designer towards the material he undertakes to shape. (11/13pt)

Efxg (36pt)

Monotype Times New Roman

The success of any process of design depends upon a sympathetic attitude on the part of the designer towards the material he undertakes to shape. The material, when its conditions are understood and met, itself meets the designer halfway. (8/9.5pt)

The success of any process of design depends upon a sympathetic attitude on the part of the designer towards the material he undertakes to shape. (11/13pt)

Efxg (36pt)

Linotype Times Ten

The success of any process of design depends upon a sympathetic attitude on the part of the designer towards the material he undertakes to shape. The material, when its conditions are understood and met, itself meets the designer halfway. (8/9.5pt)

The success of any process of design depends upon a sympathetic attitude on the part of the designer towards the material he undertakes to shape. (11/13pt)

Efxg (36pt)

Times shows the problem caused by Adobe's choice of the 18 pt Linotype version of the face as their standard. This version of the Times typeface was designed for setting at 18 pt and above. As a result it is a narrow, tightly fitted face,that gives a cramped condensed appearance when set smaller than 11 pt. At small sizes the characters are too close together, and the serifs have insufficient prominence to produce readable word profiles. Typesetters used to setting Times were relieved when Monotype Times New Roman and Linotype Times Ten became available, as these were drawn for reproduction at 6–12 pt sizes. (See p. 45 for an explanation of point sizes.)

The same shape exists only in relation to the space around it. The same line has a totally different effect in a large or small area of white space.

The same shape exists only in relation to the space around it. The same line has a totally different effect in a large or small area of white space.

Sabon shows two variants from manufacturers who have chosen to emphasize different aspects of the original metal typeface in their digital versions. Linotype (upper) has elected to emphasize the vertically stressed, sharply cut larger sizes, while Monotype (lower) has produced a typeface with a smaller x-height and more space between characters, which emphasizes the horizontal flow of the text.

g g

Remarkably similar typefaces can be disguised by different names. Monotype's Headline Bold and Font Bureau's Grotesque 37 are both based on the metal design Grotesque No. 9 by the Stephenson Blake foundry. The Monotype design (*above left*) has replaced the original g with a more restrained version; Font Bureau has retained the perkier character.

Fonts within a typeface

Roman

Italic

Roman indicates the normal upright form of a typeface, but confusingly it is also a name implying that a typeface has serifs. It is also part of the name of some typefaces, e.g. Times New Roman.

Italic is a cursive form characterized in seriffed typefaces by variant letter forms (such as *a, g, f*); an angle of slope (which varies from typeface to typeface); and by usually appearing lighter or narrower than the roman. In sans serif typefaces (and a few seriffed ones) the italic may resemble, or indeed be, the roman simply slanted. This is a failing of many of these typefaces. Italics which are slanted forms of the roman font are less successful in text setting than those which are separately drawn: this is because the weight of a word set in italic will be insufficiently distinguishable from the surrounding roman text. A slanted roman on its own, in display, looks

REPRIEVE for Transvaal lawyer

Monotype Garamond original italic shows an extreme variation in angle and slope from letter to letter.

Joanna roman and its narrow *italic*

Monotype Joanna italic is hardly sloped at all, and is mainly differentiated from the roman by its much narrower width.

flabby and uninteresting in comparison with a true-drawn italic.

Producing a heavier weight of type for emphasis means thickening up some of, but not necessarily all, the strokes of the normal weight. Most sans serifs have a bold where there is an overall thickening, and the shape of individual letters is retained from one weight to another. Making a successful bold for a seriffed typeface is not so easy, because only those strokes which are thick in the normal weight can be made considerably heavier in the bold. This is why sans serifs can be designed with large numbers of variant weights, but many seriffed typefaces come in a restricted range of weights. Bold fonts are more successful when they are slightly wider than the roman equivalent.

Bold

Old Style and **Old Style Bold**

JJ a**a** g**g**

Times New Roman, **Times Bold**
Times New Roman Medium

The idea of a 'companion bold' is a relatively recent one. Some typefaces (such as Monotype Old Style) still have bold fonts which are in a different idiom from the roman. Times Bold is also an unusual bold because the thickening up takes place only inside the letter forms; Monotype Times Medium is a variant based on a more even thickening up of the roman.

Seriffed bold italics can easily lose the elegance that makes the italic appealing, and present a sprawling appearance. These faces are best used when a variant (e.g. a foreign word) is required within a text set in bold.

Bold italic

Linotype Centennial 45
Linotype Centennial 55
Linotype Centennial 65
Linotype Centennial 75

Typefaces designed earlier this century primarily for book-work usually have only a single bold (sometimes called semi-bold) variant: more recent designs, e.g. Linotype Centennial, feature a range of bolds. There is no standardization of name to weight – the 'bold' of one typeface may be the equivalent to the 'black' of another. The system of numbering weights, where 55 is the normal roman and higher numbers indicate darker variants, smaller numbers lighter variants, is the closest approach to a logical system that exists.

SMALL CAPITALS

Small capitals in seriffed typefaces follow the shapes of capital letters, but are redrawn to match the x-height and weight of lower case letters. This means that true small capitals are both relatively wider and more strongly drawn than normal capitals. Simply shrinking capital letters does not produce adequate small capitals, although this is what most dtp applications do. To avoid this, use a font of small capitals (in PostScript typefaces also called an *expert set* or *expert collection*).

1234567890

Small capitals are a traditional form of subtle emphasis in book composition. They are usually associated with figures known as *old style* or *non-ranging*. Although these figures all sit on the baseline, they do not have a common height: 1, 2, and 0 match the x-height, 3, 4, 5, 7, and 9 are descenders, and 6 and 8 are ascenders. These figures are best for book composition, where figures should blend in to the general flow of upper and lower case text. They are usually avoided in newspaper and scientific setting, where they can look precious or confusing. An alternative is to use a typeface where figures are shorter than the capital height, such as Hell Swift or Adobe Minion.

LETTERSPACED
SMALL CAPS

UNSPACED SMALL CAPS

Small capitals achieve a greater prominence in headings in display, and will look more stylish, if spaces smaller than those used between words are inserted between the letters. This is called *letterspacing*, now more usually *tracking* on dtp applications.

Superior figures ([1234567890]) are smaller figures positioned above the x-height for use as note references etc. Expert sets and collections include true-drawn superiors, which look clearer than normal figures shrunk and repositioned electronically (sometimes called *superscript*).

Recognizing typefaces

All typefaces have particularly characteristic letters. Some of these 'earmark' characters are shown in Part II of this book. Learn to recognize the general style and weight of a typeface, and to spot these earmark characters. Identifying typefaces may be the typographical equivalent of trainspotting, but it will help you decide whether a typeface has been used appropriately or not, and help you develop your own ideas on typeface choice.

SMALL CAPS 12345
SMALL CAPS 12345
SMALL CAPS 12345
SMALL CAPS 12345
SMALL CAPS 12345
SMALL CAPS 12345
SMALL CAPS 1234
SMALL CAPS 12345

Historically, only seriffed typefaces had true small capitals and non-ranging numerals, and small caps existed only in roman form. This means you may find that although non-ranging numerals are available to match all eight Bembo variants shown above, only the roman small caps are true designs: all the others are electronic distortions of the capitals of the relevant font.

4

How do typographic measurements work?

Printing developed before national and international measuring systems were standardized, and therefore had to create its own system of measurement. Desktop publishing applications allow users to employ the metric and UK/US inch system, but the traditional printer's measurements need to be explained because some dimensions are still exclusively given in these units.

The units that are used

The basic typographic measurement is the *point* (the abbreviation is pt). This unit originally did not relate in a tidy mathematical way to either Anglo-American or to metric units. Desktop publishing has changed the definition of the point from its traditional value of 1/72.272 inch to an exact 1/72 inch. The new definition is convenient in the United States, where inches are used for paper sizes and illustration measurements, but is frustrating elsewhere because it does not relate to metric units, and has made inaccurate those typescales (rulers) marked in traditional points. In the measurement of type sizes, points are the only unit used, but the traditional unit for measuring the width and depth of an area of type is the *pica*, a pica consisting of 12 points. A measurement containing the two units (e.g. 2 picas 3 points) can be written as 2p3. Dtp systems usually allow a dimension to be entered in points (27pts) which will be converted automatically into picas and points (2p3). This shorthand is gradually displacing the older '2 1/4 picas' which cannot be entered on a computer keyboard.

Paper sizes are not defined in points and picas, and there is a strong argument for using millimetres (or inches) for all page elements (margins, gutters, column widths),

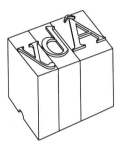

The point size of a piece of metal type included space for descenders, ascenders, and sometimes accents.

keeping points only as a measurement of the type size. There is little sense in grappling with an unfamiliar measuring system for items that can be measured in familiar units.

Measuring type

There are two vertical measurements which describe the size of a line of type, and its position in relation to the next line. The first, the *nominal point size*, is always given in points, but the second, the *line spacing* (also called the *leading* – pronounced as in 'led', not 'lead' – in dtp) can be given in points or millimetres or inches. It is important to understand exactly what is being measured when the nominal point size is stated because the measuring convention dates from letterpress typography, when types were relief letters cast in metal. The nominal point size was then simply defined: it was the height of the piece of metal on which the character sat. The amount of metal above and below the tallest ascending character and

This type is on a line spacing of 10.5 pt. Position the marks on the depth scale against the bottom line of most characters (called the *baseline*, see p. 46) until they align all the way down the column.

A depth scale (*far left*) is more useful than a typescale (*left*) because line spacing can easily be checked to 1/2 pt accuracy. Drawing layouts with correctly positioned lines of type is also very much easier.

Each

This height is the capital height.

axiom

This distance, the x-height, is the most significant factor in how big a typeface appears on the page.

align

This is the baseline.

A park

This distance, the ascender–descender or k–p height, is usually slightly less than the nominal point size. It is often slightly greater than capital–descender height.

prejudice difference

This distance is the line spacing (or baseline–baseline distance). It is usually greater than the nominal point size: when nominal size and line feed are the same, successive lines of type will usually seem barely to clear each other.

A text set in 10 pt with 12 pt line spacing is usually written 10/12 pt (spoken 'ten on twelve point').

deepest descending character varied from design to design, and this irrational system has been taken over into digital typography, so that it is almost impossible to determine the exact point size of a piece of typesetting without reference to specimens of that particular typeface at stated sizes. One aspect has been standardized since metal days: when set in a line, all fonts share a common *baseline* (metal types of different designs did not align in this way).

Types with large and small x-heights

Although all typefaces have a common baseline, the proportions of *x-height*, *capital height*, *ascender* and *descender height* vary enormously from face to face. All the extremities of any character in a typeface must fit within the nominal point size, and the most obvious difference between typefaces is the relative proportion of the x-height. Those with a large x-height are said to have a large *appearing size*.

The only sure way to identify and check nominal point sizes is to print out examples for each size you intend to use and label them clearly for reference: it will help if you use the same nominal size on a variety of line spacings. This will give you a known reference, and let you judge the appearing size of each font, which is visually more significant than the nominal size.

It is important to print these samples, and not rely on screen displays! As 1pt = 1 screen pixel it is impossible to compare the true appearances of particular point sizes on screen.

Monotype Century Schoolbook

The same shape exists only in relation to the space around it. The same line has a totally different effect in a large or a small area of white space (10/10 pt, also expressed as '10 pt solid')

The same shape exists only in relation to the space around it. The same line has a totally different effect in a large or a small area of white space (11/11 pt)

The same shape exists only in relation to the space around it. The same line has a totally different effect in a large or a small area of white space (10/11 pt)

The same shape exists only in relation to the space around it. The same line has a totally different effect in a large or a small area of white space (11/12 pt)

The same shape exists only in relation to the space around it. The same line has a totally different effect in a large or a small area of white space (10/12 pt)

The same shape exists only in relation to the space around it. The same line has a totally different effect in a large or a small area of white space (11/13 pt)

Prepare a specimen sheet to verify nominal sizes, or use a utility like TypeBook to produce one for you. When using such a specimen to choose

a point size and line spacing it is important to change as few variables as possible between examples.

Centaur in 36 pt looks smaller than Nimrod in 36 pt

Appearing size is visually more significant than nominal point size. It is usually related to the x-height, although the overall heaviness of a design is also a contributory factor.

Nimrod set in 12 pt on 12 pt line spacing looks crowded because the space between each line is smaller than the x-height of each line.

12/12 pt Centaur has smaller, less visible letter forms but does not require additional leading as much as the adjacent Nimrod sample.

6 pt Nimrod is quite readable.

6 pt Centaur almost disappears

The relationship between nominal point size and line spacing

As a rule, typefaces with a large x-height will perform better at smaller sizes than those with a smaller x-height. Size for size, Nimrod outperforms Centaur for visibility at 6, 7, and 8 pt. This is where careful consideration of line spacing becomes necessary. Because the ratio of x-height to nominal point size is so large, Nimrod has a clogged appearance when set over a wider measure if the line spacing is not large enough.

Getting the line spacing right is one of the fundamentals of good typographic design. Just as indifferently drawn letters can be redeemed if the allocation of space between letters is done with care, so the blandest of typefaces can look comfortable and inviting to read if sufficient leading is given. This means that the space between the x-heights of succeeding lines must be greater than the x-heights themselves. In wider columns line spacing needs to be increased, to help the eye return easily to the start of the following line. In text sizes of 9 to 12 pt across column widths of about 100 mm, 15–30 per cent of the point size is an appropriate amount. (The type of this text is 10 pt, on a line spacing of 12.5 pt.) Typefaces always benefit from leading, even in a narrow column.

The meaning of the word *leading* has changed since the days of metal type. Originally leads (pronounced 'leds') were strips of metal inserted between lines of type to open it out to the appropriate line spacing: 10 pt type could be '2 pt leaded' to give a 12 pt line spacing.

Leading was the addition to the nominal size which gave the final baseline–baseline distance, not the baseline–baseline distance itself. Leading is used in this book with its traditional meaning: total baseline–baseline distance is called *line spacing*.

Proportional leading

As well as allowing you to define nominal point size and line spacing independently, many dtp applications have an *automatic* line spacing setting. This defines a proportion of the current point size to which the line spacing is set, without having to be entered by the user. For example, an automatic value of 120 per cent will set 10 pt type on a 12 pt line spacing, and this ratio will be constant for all other sizes.

You will need to assess whether the automatic line spacing values are suitable for the typeface, size, and column width you have selected: 20 per cent, for example, might be suitable for column widths of 100 mm and a typeface of 'normal' x-height proportions such as Times, but insufficient for a face with a very large x-height such as Antique Olive.

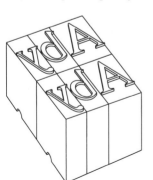

How do typographic measurements work?

Proportional leading: 20 per cent is added to the point size to give the line spacing. Larger sizes can appear excessively spaced.

Constant value leading: here 2 points are added to the point size to give the line spacing value throughout the size range. This can produce over-spaced small type, and cramped larger sizes.

Optically equalized leading: line feed values are calculated individually, increasing less than proportionately as the point size increases. This system can give the most even 'colour' to a page.

Monotype Plantin: 8, 10, 14, 18, 24 pt

8/10, 10/12, 14/16, 18/20, 24/26 pt

8/9, 10/12, 14/16, 18/21, 24/27 pt

The success of any process of design depends upon a sympathetic attitude on the part of the designer towards the material he undertakes to shape. The material, when its conditions are understood and met, itself meets the designer half way.

The success of any process of design depends upon a sympathetic attitude on the part of the designer towards the material he undertakes to shape. The material, when its conditions are understood and met, itself meets the designer half way.

The success of any process of design depends upon a sympathetic attitude on the part of the designer towards the material he undertakes to shape. The material, when its conditions are understood and met, itself meets the designer half way.

The success of any process of design depends upon a sympathetic attitude on the part of the designer towards the material he undertakes to shape.

The success of any process of design depends upon a sympathetic attitude on the part of the designer towards the material he undertakes to shape.

The success of any process of design depends upon a sympathetic attitude on the part of the designer towards the material he undertakes to shape.

The success of any process of design depends upon a sympathetic attitude on the part of the

The success of any process of design depends upon a sympathetic attitude on the part of the

The success of any process of design depends upon a sympathetic attitude on the part of the

The success of any process of design

The success of any process of design

The success of any process of design

The success of any process of design depends

The success of any process of design depends

The success of any process of design depends

How do typographic measurements work?

This is 14 pt Bembo on 16 pt, a conventional printer's nominal point size/line spacing combination.

Although dtp systems usually display line spacing values in points, it may be easier to define this distance in millimetres,

This is 14 pt Bembo on a line spacing of 6mm, which allows me to tell instantly that 20 lines will fit into my column depth of 120 mm.

Same name, different x-heights

We saw in chapter 3 that different manufacturers' versions of the same design had different x-heights and k–p dimensions at the same output size. This has an effect on the line spacing needed to produce equivalent amounts of white space between the lines of type (called *interlinear white*). In Sabon, Linotype's characters occupy more of the nominal height than Monotype's. Setting both at 12/14 pt (see below) will result not only in different appearing sizes, but also, because of the different amounts of interlinear white, in a difference in what typographers call the colour or texture of the page. Remember to go by specimens of the typefaces you are using, rather than other typesetters' specimens.

The typeface examples in this book show up a further problem that dtp users should be aware of: fonts from different manufacturers with the same name have different k–p dimensions and x-height.

Sabon shows two variants from manufacturers who have chosen to emphasize different aspects of the original hot-metal typeface in their digital versions. Linotype has elected to emphasize the vertically stressed, sharply cut larger sizes, while Monotype has produced a horizontally stressed, darker typeface. Linotype Sabon 12/14 pt.

Sabon shows two variants from manufacturers who have chosen to emphasize different aspects of the original hot-metal typeface in their digital versions. Linotype has elected to emphasize the vertically stressed, sharply cut larger sizes, while Monotype has produced a horizontally stressed, darker typeface. Monotype Sabon 12/14 pt.

Horizontal measurement

In metal type, horizontal measurement was done in picas or *ems* (an em equalled the point size, being 6 points at 6 pt, 12 points at 12 pt, etc.) and *ens* (half an em). 'Em' and 'en' are now only used to define the width of spaces and dashes. Because they can be misunderstood when spoken, printers have traditionally renamed them the *mutton* and *nut*, to avoid confusion.

Horizontal measurement of the type area can now be carried out in millimetres, inches, or picas. But the dtp application actually counts individual characters in *units of set*. The unit of set is a fraction of the point size (in PostScript fonts 1/1000th) and therefore varies in absolute size from point size to point size. Character widths are defined in units of set by the manufacturer so that the width of a character (and therefore its side-by-side placement with another) can be defined independently of output point size. Most dtp packages do not permit the user to examine or alter the actual widths of characters in a font, even when they allow you to make adjustments to the side-by-side placing of characters by *kerning* and *tracking* (see chapter 5).

Spaces, as well as characters, are defined in units of set. In text composition, a word space that is about one-quarter of an em (250 units in PostScript, about the width of the letter i) will give an even flow to the line. In metal type, spaces consisted of pieces of lead of defined sizes: they had names such as *mid*, *thick*, *thin*. Only four spaces other than the word space need to be considered in relation to dtp, however. These are the *em-space*, the *en-space*, the *figure space*, and the *punctuation space*.

aa

A character has the same unit width value whatever the output size. Both these examples of Adobe Garamond a are 404 units wide.

aa

Unit values of individual letters vary from font to font, most noticeably in condensed and expanded versions of a design.

All figures in a font are usually allocated the same unit width, so that tabular material will align vertically without adjustment. Figures are usually 500 units wide. The *en-rule* (a rule 500 units wide) is used to show an extent of figures, instead of the hyphen used in typing.

The PostScript character set allows for a *fitted* figure 1, which avoids gappiness around this character. This version should not be used in tabular matter.

1602–1945
1011–1110
1011–1110 fitted
In 1991
In 1991 fitted

Appendix 27 The Human Body

San Francisco New York Hong Kong

En-spaces can separate groups of words more emphatically than single word spaces. They are preferable to double word spaces.

Although these four spaces are called fixed spaces, it is the number of units they occupy that is fixed for a particular font, not their width in millimetres or inches. The em-space has the same width as the current point size (1000/1000 units); the en-space is half an em-space (therefore half the current point size, 500/1000 units). A 24 pt em-space is exactly 24 pts wide, a 24 pt en-space exactly 12 pts wide.

A figure space matches the width of figures in a font (italic figures may be narrower than roman, bold figures wider), and the punctuation space matches the width of the comma and full point (period).

Hong   Kong One   of Asia's largest centres of digital typesetting.

Hong Kong One of Asia's largest centres of digital typesetting.

Remember that these spaces are fixed, and if you are using justified setting, where word spaces vary from line to line, the en-space may appear smaller than the word space of a particular line.

Using fixed spaces

When defining indents it is better to stick with your preferred horizontal measurement (which you can after all measure with a ruler and input at your keyboard) rather than attempt to work with fixed spaces. The en- and em-spaces can be used when you want to introduce a space within a line of type to emphasize the grouping or separation of certain words. Figure and punctuation spaces are required to retain alignment in tabular work with figures.

 **Bargains!**

It would be useful to know how wide the fist was, so that the indent for subsequent lines could be defined exactly.

**Bargains!
Bargains!!**

Some dtp applications allow the insertion of an invisible *indent here* character to ensure this.

**Bargains!
Bargains!!**

You may need to use trial and error or resort to such dodges as repeating the character...

**Bargains!
Bargains!!**

...but in white so that its width is preserved but the character itself does not appear.

Unit values for Adobe Garamond

i 257 units   l 247 units

M 912 units

n 525 units   2 500 units

M | n

The em-space and en-space, despite their names, are often not exactly equal to the width of the m and n. The M in this font is 912 units wide , not 1000; and the n is 525 units wide, not 500.

good i tight i spacing

The widths of certain characters can be regarded as standard for a font. For close word spacing the unit width of the i or l may represent a good choice for the word space.

The punctuation space represents the width of the comma and full point and may be necessary to preserve alignments in column work using figure groups divided by commas and full points.

The figure space allows vertical alignment of figures when tabs are either unavailable or impractical.

The figure space varies from font to font: it can be larger than, the same as, or smaller than the true en-space, depending on whether the figures are narrower or wider.

123 123

2 300 70 francs
£1,322.40

1234
234
123
2 4

If you need to calculate the space allowance for figures, start on the assumption that they are 500 units wide.

5

What are the different ways of setting type?

The width to which a line of type can be set is limited because there is a natural limit to the distance the eye can travel efficiently along a line. Reading consists, not of focusing on every letter or word, but of a series of intermittent sweeps by the eye along the line of type, with pauses for focusing. The eye can focus on only a small group of letters or words and perceives the immediately surrounding words less clearly. We recognize familiar word profiles. This is why a text in capitals and small letters is less tiring to read than a text set only in capitals.

We understand what we are reading from a combination of what we see clearly and what we guess from the context. Long lines cause problems: they require too many pauses along a line and slow down reading speed, because we literally lose our way. We return to check words we have just read, or start to focus on every word; long lines also makes the eye's return sweep more likely to pick up the wrong line to read next.

Experience suggests a line length, for a standard-format book, of about ten words or 50–60 characters. Clearly, a newspaper column contains fewer words, and often a single-column page of A4 format or larger may contain many more. Fortunately there are ways of maximizing readability in most cases. The practical readability of all these column widths is directly affected by the apparent size of the type and the apparent vertical space between lines. Controlling the horizontal spacing of words is also important because spacing that is too tight will make the word profiles run together, and spacing that is too loose will reduce the amount we can absorb at each pause along the line.

Columns

Type that is to be read continuously is rarely spattered across the page: regular alignments at left and (less often) right are a constant feature of typographic design. The number of columns to a page is a fair guide to the potential complexity of the page; indeed, certain columnar arrangements are so closely identified with specific kinds of texts that they are immediately recognizable.

Alignments

Almost all typeset matter uses the left-hand edge of the column as the key alignment point. This is not surprising, as we read from left to right and the eye must travel back to a clear starting point to pick up the next line for reading. A strong alignment at the left allows considerable variation, called *indenting*, to be given to certain lines to differentiate them: this can be done either to all the lines in a paragraph after the first, or with the first line being given special treatment.

(*Top left*) All lines with equal left margin causes ambiguity when the last line of a paragraph is not visibly shorter than the others. Increased line spacing is necessary, as in the text of this book.

(*Top centre*) First line of paragraphs indented. An em-space is the most normal indent, but it can be increased in very wide columns. The first paragraph under a heading should not be indented.

(*Top right*) First lines of paragraphs *hang*, i.e. extend further to the left than subsequent lines.

(*Bottom left*) Whole paragraph differentiated by indent. Note the use of additional line spacing above and below.

(*Bottom centre*) Multiple levels of text indicated by indents. Note the use of headings and bulleted points to break up the text.

Benefits of computerized typography

Digital type at high resolution has banished fuzzy edges from type. Font formats which use mathematical descriptions of curves have rescued letterforms from straight line segments. We are promised non-linear scaling, to adjust the relative proportions of x-height to ascenders and descenders, and thick to thin stroke ratios.

But it is the transition of typographic form from an industrial craft to a post-industrial craft that offers designers the most scope. Typography and computing have become inseparable, to the benefit of both. And now typography moves with the flow of computer developments, in the fastest stream.

A decade ago typographic software was custom-built; now it can be bought off the shelf, shrink-wrapped. Control of typographic standards was erratic when designers' instructions had to pass through the hands of computer programmers.

Benefits of computerized typography

Digital type at high resolution has banished fuzzy edges from type. Font formats which use mathematical descriptions of curves have rescued letterforms from straight line segments. We are promised non-linear scaling, to adjust the relative proportions of x-height to ascenders and descenders, and thick to thin stroke ratios.

But it is the transition of typographic form from an industrial craft to a post-industrial craft that offers designers the most scope. Typography and computing have become inseparable, to the benefit of both. And typography moves with the flow of computer developments, in the fastest stream.

A decade ago typographic software was custom-built; now it can be bought off the shelf, shrink-wrapped. Control of typographic standards was erratic when designers' instructions had to pass through the hands of computer

Benefits of computerized typography

Digital type at high resolution has banished fuzzy edges from type. Font formats which use mathematical descriptions of curves have rescued letterforms from straight line segments. We are promised non-linear scaling, to adjust the relative proportions of x-height to ascenders and descenders, and thick to thin stroke ratios.

But it is the transition of typographic form from an industrial craft to a post-industrial craft that offers designers the most scope. Typography and computing have become inseparable, to the benefit of both. And now typography moves with the flow of computer developments, in the fastest stream.

A decade ago typographic software was custom-built; now it can be bought off the shelf, shrink-wrapped. Control of typographic standards was erratic when designers' instructions had to pass through the hands of computer programmers.

Benefits of computerized typography

Digital type at high resolution has banished fuzzy edges from type.

Font formats which use mathematical descriptions of curves have rescued letterforms from straight line segments.

We are promised

- non-linear scaling
- ability to alter character set
- transformation from one format to another

Changes in status

The transition of typographic form from an industrial craft to a post-industrial craft that offers designers the most scope.

Typography and computing have become inseparable, to the benefit of both.

Typography moves with the flow of computer developments, in the fastest stream.

Benefits of computerized typography

Digital type at high resolution has banished fuzzy edges from type. Font formats which use mathematical descriptions of curves have rescued letterforms from straight line segments. We are promised non-linear scaling, to adjust the relative proportions of x-height to ascenders and descenders, and thick to thin stroke ratios. We are promised non-linear scaling, to adjust the relative proportions of x-height to ascenders and descenders, and thick to thin stroke ratios.

But it is the transition of typographic form from an industrial craft to a post-industrial craft that offers designers the most scope. Typography and computing have become inseparable, to the benefit of both. And typography moves with the flow of computer developments, in the fastest stream.

A decade ago typographic software was custom-built; now it can be bought off the shelf, shrink-wrapped. Control of typographic standards was erratic when designers' instructions had to pass through the hands of computer programmers.

If the importance of the left-hand edge of a column for ease of reading is obvious, the case for a regular right-hand edge is less clear-cut. Alignment at both left and right (*justified* setting) was once seen as the feature that made typesetting look different from typewriting. Justification is not, however, a necessary aid to legibility, and is achieved by means which may actually make the text less readable. Unless the width of the column (the *measure* in traditional terminology) is extremely wide, a regular right-hand edge will mean that the spaces between words vary, sometimes significantly, and that to avoid excessive variation words at the end of the line must sometimes be divided.

The narrow column example (*below left*), set in 12/15 pt across 57 mm, has an average of 30 characters per line. Word spacing varies erratically from line to line. The wider column (*below*), set across 119 mm, has an average of 65 characters per line, and far less varied word spacing.

Digital type at high resolution has banished fuzzy edges from type. Font formats which use mathematical descriptions of curves have rescued letterforms from straight line segments. We are promised non-linear scaling, to adjust the relative proportions of x-height to ascenders and descenders, and thick to thin stroke ratios.

But it is the transition of typographic form from an industrial craft to a post-industrial craft

Digital type at high resolution has banished fuzzy edges from type. Font formats which use mathematical descriptions of curves have rescued letterforms from straight line segments. We are promised non-linear scaling, to adjust the relative proportions of x-height to ascenders and descenders, and thick to thin stroke ratios.

But it is the transition of typographic form from an industrial craft to a post-industrial craft that offers designers the most scope. Typography and computing have become inseparable, to the benefit of both. And typography moves with the flow of computer developments, in the fastest stream.

A decade ago typographic software was custom-built; now it can be bought off the shelf, shrink-wrapped. Control of typographic standards was erratic when designers' instructions had to pass through the hands of computer programmers.

Hyphenation and justification

The computer routine that determines the horizontal spacing of words is called *hyphenation and justification* (h&j). There are four ways a column can be composed: three involve fixed spaces between words (left, right, and centred alignments); the fourth, justified setting, uses variable word spaces, as we have seen. Left-aligned and justified are the only practical styles for continuous reading, because only they provide the all-important constant left-hand edge. Left-aligned setting is also called *ragged* setting.

Before h&j can be performed on a text, certain starting points have to be established: the preferred space between words, which will become the only space used in ragged setting; the minimum and maximum word spaces that will be allowed in justified setting; whether word division is permitted, and with what rules. (Although word division is almost always a necessity in justified setting, it is available in ragged setting too.)

Choosing the appropriate h&j values

The spacing between words needs to be chosen with as much care as the size of type, the width of line, and the space between lines. This is because the clarity of a piece of typesetting depends on the interaction of all these variables. The ideal h&j routine for a text will give word spacing that is consistently less than the apparent space between lines, but related to the width of the characters in the font being set, and to the spaces that the manufacturer has allocated between letters.

Typesetting systems should put control of typography in the hands of the designer, not because he has the aesthetic sensibility to arrange display type, or to choose a striking typeface, but because the designer should be the guardian of readability. If the designer is elevated from a specifier to an implementer, he may realize how much care the craftsmen of

Ragged without hyphenation.

Typesetting systems should put control of typography in the hands of the designer, not because he has the aesthetic sensibility to arrange display type, or choose a striking typeface, but because the designer should be the guardian of readability. If the designer is elevated from a specifier to an implementer, he may realize how much care the craftsmen of the

Ragged with hyphenation.

Typesetting systems should put control of typography in the hands of the designer, not because he has the aesthetic sensibility to arrange display type, or to choose a striking typeface, but because the designer should be the guardian of readability. If the designer is elevated from a specifier to an implementer, he may realize how much care the craftsmen of

Justified without hyphenation.

Typesetting systems should put control of typography in the hands of the designer, not because he has the aesthetic sensibility to arrange display type, or to choose a striking typeface, but because the designer should be the guardian of readability. If the designer is elevated from a specifier to an implementer, he may realize how much care the craftsmen of the

Justified with hyphenation.

You can have several 'h&j's within a document: one which gives wider word spaces for smaller type sizes or for characters which have more space between them; another for larger sizes of type, or for those fonts which are narrow and tightly spaced. Fortunately, applications such as Aldus PageMaker or Quark XPress are supplied already set up with h&j values that are close enough to the norm for professional text composition to make adjustment a matter of refinement rather than necessity. (Such preset but adjustable settings are called *defaults*.) This is not the case with some word processing applications, where excessively wide word spacing is still normal.

The h&j routine calculates the width of these word spaces in units of set, not points or millimetres. (For a definition of units of set see p. 51.) Unfortunately, dtp applications do not allow the user to define these spaces directly in units of set. Some call for obscure definitions: for example, Quark XPress asks you to enter values as a 'percentage of the defined space of the font', but nowhere is this 'defined space' documented. Manufacturers' standards vary – some of Monotype's 'defined spaces' seem wider than ideal, some of Linotype's tighter. Reaching a desired space, e.g. the width of the letter i, can only be achieved through trial and error. You will need to check your application and see whether the default is appropriate or should be adjusted.

The same shape exists only in relation to the space around it. The same line has a totally different effect in a large or small area of white space.

Typesetting systems should put control of typography in the hands of the designer, not because he has the aesthetic sensibility to arrange display type, or to choose a striking typeface, but because the designer should be the guardian of readability. If the designer is elevated from a specifier to an implementer, he may realize how much care the craftsmen of the past put into the composition of their pages, and be inspired

(*Top left*) Centaur italic (more correctly called Arrighi) set with narrow word spaces (160 PostScript units).

(*Top right*) Small size of Imprint with wider word spaces (333 units).

(*Bottom left*) Frutiger bold set with normal word spaces (250 units).

(*Bottom right*) Large size of Helvetica Compressed with narrower word spaces (160 units).

The same shape exists only in relation to the space around it. The same line has a totally different

The same shape exists only in relation to the space around it. The same line has

59

Letterspacing

One alteration to any preset values is strongly recommended: h&j routines may include an attempt to adjust spaces between characters to avoid excessive spacing between words. This is undesirable because the profiles of words, so important for legibility, will suffer; and because consecutive lines of type will have different apparent weights (the extra spacing dilutes the visual density of the line). A word of warning: variation of character spacing is rarely detectable on screen.

Deliberate *letterspacing* (now more generally called *tracking*) is an effective way of equalizing the visual spacing of capitals, or of adjusting the overall spacing of characters by very small amounts (see p. 67).

CENTAUR TYPE

CENTAUR TYPE

Traditional letterspacing is used to improve the rhythm of lines set entirely in capitals, which look crowded when set unspaced. Letterspacing also reduces the effect of inconsistent spacing between particular character combinations, such as NTAU and TYP above.

Digital type at high resolution has banished fuzzy edges from type. Font formats which use mathematical descriptions of curves have rescued letterforms from straight line segments. We are promised non-linear scaling, to adjust the relative proportions of x-height to ascenders and descenders, and thick to thin stroke ratios.

But it is the transition of typographic form from an industrial craft to a post-industrial craft that offers designers the most scope. Typography and computing have become inseparable, to the benefit of both. And typography moves with the flow of computer developments, in the fastest stream.

A decade ago typographic software was custom-built; now it can be bought off the shelf, shrink-wrapped. Control of typographic standards was erratic when designers' instructions had to pass through the hands of computer programmers.

Allowing the h&j routine to adjust character spaces leads to the style of setting shown above, where character spacing varies from line to line, constantly dazzling the reader. The last paragraph shows the effect of allowing character spaces to be reduced as well as increased.

Word division

Word division becomes necessary in justified setting when the column width (and average length of words) would otherwise make the spaces between words excessively wide.

In the same way that the preferred word space varies, so what constitutes excessive word space will also vary, but certainly word spacing that exceeds an em-space will look too wide in any context.

Word division is never entirely satisfactory, unless the word is itself a compound (e.g. horse-shoe). Applications claim to divide words correctly, but often fail to do so. Word division should be unobtrusive to the reader, who should not be stopped short by a puzzling (or offensive) division. Word division was historically done by compositors and readers on the basis of the etymology of the word: the Greek, Latin, and French origins of the word would be taken into account, as in photo-grapher . This is still the style of the university presses, and many academic publishers. More common among word processing applications (and newspapers) is to divide by splitting between two consonants (photog-raphy), or the simple removal of prefix and suffix (photograph-er).

Word division routines can be amended by the user to avoid repeated problems. It is difficult to give general advice to users on making such amendments. One overriding rule, however, can be given: the first part of the divided word should unambiguously suggest the second. *The Oxford Minidictionary of Spelling* attempts to follow this rule and gives word division points for some 90,000 words, selected pragmatically; it provides a useful check when an application's word division feels wrong.

Capitalized words

The division of words with initial capital letter may be problematic in a text which contains many names: these need particular checking, and exceptions to the program's default need to be created when they divide unpleasantly (Mac-namara is better than Macna-mara). Special care has to be taken with foreign names.

Controlling the amount of word division that an h&j routine applies is obviously important: the more word division there is, the more even the word spacing, but the greater the number of possible hesitations for the reader. Traditional book composition aimed for as few as one or two divided words per page. Checking and if necessary adjusting the following defaults will give you greater control, but you may still find that an individual piece of text needs local adjustment on a paragraph by paragraph basis.

Consecutive hyphens

Two consecutive hyphens are the maximum allowed in traditional book composition but three are certainly acceptable in newspaper-style columns. Increasing the number will result in confusing runs of hyphens, with the danger that the reader will lose track of which line to read next.

Minimum character requirements

You should be able to select how many letters a word has before it is eligible for division, and also how many characters should remain before the line-end hyphen, and how many can be taken over to the next line. Setting high values for all of these variables will obviously reduce the incidence of word division, as the h&j routine will find fewer acceptable division points. In general narrow columns require more division points than wider ones.

Very short words should not be divided, especially if they are of one syllable or of four letters or less (mica, very). A working guide would be to select six characters as the minimum length of word eligible for division (so un-tidy would divide but af-ter would be forbidden).

A minimum of two characters before the hyphen is suitable for narrow-to-medium length columns (allowing words to be divided after un-, ex-, in-). This is less appropriate for longer line lengths, where three or even four characters may be a better choice, ensuring inter-national and under-ground rather than in-ternational and un-derground.

A minimum of two characters after the hyphen permits auth-or and free-ly, but again produces too many possible division points for anything but the narrowest column widths. A limit of three characters, which allows -ing and -ion to be taken over, is more normal for medium-to-wider column widths.

It is important to weigh up whether word division or excessive amounts of white space at the ends of some lines are preferable. An experiment with ragged setting without word division in the London *Observer* in the 1960s was criticised by readers for apparently casting columnist Katharine Whitehorn into blank verse: when the London *Guardian* introduced wholesale ragged setting with word division in 1988 this criticism was not heard, as line endings showed considerably less variation.

The success of any process of design depends upon a sympathetic attitude on the part of the designer towards the material he undertakes to shape. The material, when its conditions are understood, itself meets the designer halfway.

The success of any process of design depends upon a sympathetic attitude on the part of the designer towards the material he undertakes to shape. The material, when its conditions are understood, itself meets the designer halfway.

Presi-dent flies back to Washing-ton

Bush returns to White House

Headlines are never hyphenated in newspapers; great care is taken to write copy which fits the space available. But one does see excessive inter-word spaces when hyphenation is not allowed in the text.

The
Music
of
Shake-
speare

This would be acceptable on the narrow spine of a book, but not across the width of a title page.

When to allow word division

Word division is almost always necessary in continuous justified text, but this is not the case with ragged setting. Here it is possible to avoid word division, if greater variation of line length is acceptable. The same h&j values that produce an acceptable level of hyphenation in justified setting will produce more frequent hyphenation in ragged setting, so adjustments should be made.

Word division should be avoided in larger type sizes and in headings because it destroys word profiles and reduces the instant recognition of text that is intended as a signal rather than as connected prose. You can avoid this problem by defining different h&j routines for use in headings and text.

It is better to break headings according to sense than to allow part of a single word to make a new line.

Technology breakout session: computerizing a national news-paper

This session is open to all delegates who have indicated this choice on their booking form. A coach will be available to take delegates to the Docklands printing works of the *Financial Times*.

Technology breakout session: computerizing a national newspaper

This session is open to all delegates who have indicated this choice on their booking form. A coach will be available to take delegates to the Docklands printing works of the *Financial Times*.

Choosing word division points

You can override the automatic logic of h&j routines and define a particular division by inserting a *discretionary hyphen*, or by entering a specific division in an *exception dictionary*. The former will be acted upon only when that instance is encountered; adding to or changing the dictionary will affect every occurrence of that word. Amend dictionaries with care: remember to consider plural or past tense forms when entering a word.

Choosing between justified and ragged setting

As we have noted, justified setting is not necessarily more legible than ragged setting, and carries the penalty of almost always requiring word division. Ragged setting should therefore have a greater usefulness, and has become increasingly acceptable over the past fifty years; but it is still avoided, for historical and aesthetic rather than practical reasons, in most book and newspaper composition. Justified text with centred headings will always represent a formal, traditional approach, while ragged setting and headings will have the potential for informality and modernity.

Multiple alignments

Sometimes a document is so complex that a variety of alignments is required to clarify the text. Simplicity is always the best approach. The left-hand sample shows a traditional approach, often categorized as symmetrical: centred, justified, and left-aligned setting are all used, with the aim of producing a formal design, ideally balanced on the axis of a double page spread. The right-hand example shows an asymmetrical approach, using only left-aligned setting.

The examples (*right*) show something of the atmosphere value of centred and left-aligned setting, showing how this can reinforce other typographic choices, such as that between seriffed and sans serif typefaces (see p. 74) and between formal and informal typefaces (see p. 84).

Design/Technology/Communication Conference

Optional session: Design for Print

Putting the craft back into book design

Paul Luna

ABSTRACT

Attitudes to craft which are based on aesthetic considerations and nostalgia are rejected in favour of analysis of features by which compositors and printers' readers made the texts they handled more readable. The case is argued for designers to use desktop publishing to implement design as well as specify for it.

Why should we want to put the craft back into design? Surely design in the 1990s is in reaction against artiness and craftiness? Isn't the craft tradition of fine books,[1] deluxe editions,[2] and hand-presses a dead end that the modern designer wants to avoid?

In book composition the aspects of craft I want to reinstate are those which assist the reader through the text. These can be summarized as: appropriate character spacing; appropriate word spacing; appropriate line end decisions; appropriate page end decisions.

1 William Morris, *Works of Chaucer*, 1896
2 Bruce Rogers, *Utopia*, 1932

Design/Technology/Communication Conference

Optional session: Design for Print

Putting the craft back into book design

Paul Luna

ABSTRACT   Attitudes to craft which are based on aesthetic considerations and nostalgia are rejected in favour of analysis of features by which compositors and printers' readers made the texts they handled more readable. The case is argued for designers to use desktop publishing to implement design as well as specify for it.

Why should we want to put the craft back into design? Surely design in the 1990s is in reaction against artiness and craftiness? Isn't the craft tradition of fine books,[1] deluxe editions,[2] and hand-presses a dead end that the modern designer wants to avoid?

In book composition the aspects of craft I want to reinstate are those which assist the reader through the text. These can be summarized as: appropriate character spacing; appropriate word spacing; appropriate line end decisions; appropriate page end decisions.

1 William Morris, *Works of Chaucer*, 1896
2 Bruce Rogers, *Utopia*, 1932

Kerning and tracking

The automatic h&j routine will arrange characters using the widths allocated to each by the typeface manufacturer. These widths are based on the preferences of the typeface designer and the experience of the manufacturer. There are ways of adjusting these widths within dtp applications. These adjustments can be made on a one-off, local basis, or incorporated into the default setting of your dtp application to use whenever specified. If you wish to make adjustments to these professionally set standards, it is important to test your ideas before implementing them.

Kerning removes or inserts space between individual character pairs, and is necessary because the basic unit widths allocated at design need to cover the whole range of possible letter combinations. Without kerning, pairs such as AV, ay, To, etc. will appear to have space between them; TT, wy, etc. will appear to clash. Kerning becomes valuable when characters are set large enough for the reader to be disturbed by the apparent irregularity of spacing of the unamended font: at smaller text composition sizes (9 pt and below) too little kerning is better than too much. Kerning can be applied either by selecting a particular character pair and defining a positive or negative value (one-off kerning) or by selecting automatic implementation of the kerning pair tables throughout a particular job. Most dtp typefaces come complete with kerning information, consisting of tables which list spacing adjustments between relevant pairs of letters.

A kerning pair table is only valid for one font (because the shapes of letters vary from roman to bold to italic, as well as from typeface to typeface). You may be asked to define a minimum size above which kerning will take place. It is best not to tinker with the tables; instead manually adjust pairs which still look unsatisfactory after automatic kerning has been implemented.

minimal

minimal

minimal

minimal

minimal

minimal

minimal

minimal

minimal

minimal

minimal

minimal

Typefaces are now more tightly spaced: compare Monotype Imprint (*far left*), which is closely based on the metal version cut in 1910, and Monotype Photina, issued in1971 (*left*). Imprint represents 'traditional' spacing, which is right for 8 pt to 10 pt but looks loose at larger sizes. Photina has much less space between letters: because the typeface is well drawn, this does not cause crowding in smaller sizes, and produces good close fitting in larger sizes.

Kerning improves the fit of capital letters with diagonal strokes.

The width allocated to T avoids clashes with h: this leads to gappiness with o and a.

The width of a gives suitable spacing when surrounding characters fill the x-height.

Neighbouring characters which contain space within their width (such as r, v, w, and y) require kerning.

Compare Monotype Dante set without kerning (*below*) and kerned using the manufacturer's kerning pair tables (*bottom*).

(This book is set with all type larger than 8 pt kerned automatically, using the manufacturers' kerning pair tables.)

Tracking increases or decreases the space between all letters of a word, paragraph, or page. It has two uses: positive tracking *letterspaces* words set entirely in small capitals or capitals (see p. 68), and compensates for apparent tightness of fit at small sizes; negative tracking compensates for apparent looseness of fit at large sizes. In both cases the amount of adjustment should be very small (perhaps as little as 5–15 PostScript units) if there is not to be damage to the word profiles and the character of the typeface. As with kerning, too little tracking is preferable to too much. Tracking and kerning can be combined. (There is no tracking of the main text or headings of this book.)

JAVA
The Toy.
away,
JAVA
The Toy.
away,

5/8 pt Linotype Univers 55 tracked +10 units (*top right*) and set without tracking.

Why should we want to put the craft back into design? Surely design in the 1990s is in reaction against artiness and craftiness? Isn't the craft tradition of fine books, deluxe editions, and hand-presses a dead end that the modern designer wants to avoid?

Why should we want to put the craft back into design? Surely design in the 1990s is in reaction against artiness and craftiness? Isn't the craft tradition of fine books, deluxe editions, and hand-presses a dead end that the modern designer wants to avoid?

Monotype Imprint (*right*) tracked −20 units at 48 pt and −10 units at 36 pt. Compare with the same sizes without tracking on p. 66.

minimal
minimal

Letterspacing

In metal type, capital letter forms produced obvious gaps and near collisions unless letterspacing was added. Lines which consist entirely of seriffed capitals or small capitals should always be letterspaced: the historical rule of thumb was to add about 1/10 of an em at composition sizes, and about 1/20 of an em at display sizes. The equivalent for dtp composition is to track text size capitals by 100 PostScript units, displayed capitals by 50 units, although this will give looser spacing than is absolutely necessary; 40–80 units may be all that is needed.

These values may be difficult to define in some programs. You can use the examples below to check the values used in your program, if they are not alterable or if the units used are difficult to calculate. In general the more words to be letterspaced, the less letterspacing is needed. Sans serif typefaces and most bold fonts need little if any letterspacing.

SMALL CAPITALS NOT LETTERSPACED

SMALL CAPITALS LETTERSPACED 25 POSTSCRIPT UNITS

SMALL CAPITALS LETTERSPACED 50 POSTSCRIPT UNITS

SMALL CAPITALS LETTERSPACED 80 POSTSCRIPT UNITS

SMALL CAPITALS LETTERSPACED 100 POSTSCRIPT UNITS

SMALL CAPITALS LETTERSPACED 125 POSTSCRIPT UNITS

CAPITALS NOT LETTERSPACED

CAPITALS LETTERSPACED 25 POSTSCRIPT UNITS

CAPITALS LETTERSPACED 50 POSTSCRIPT UNITS

CAPITALS LETTERSPACED 80 POSTSCRIPT UNITS

CAPITALS LETTERSPACED 100 POSTSCRIPT UNITS

CAPITALS LETTERSPACED 125 POSTSCRIPT UNITS

100-unit letterspacing is close to the traditional hot-metal style for text-size lines of small capitals. 80-unit letterspacing is equivalent to the traditional spacing for display. 50-unit letterspacing is a useful minimum clearance for longer lines of capitals in smaller sizes. (These values are given in PostScript units, 1000 to the em. You will need to translate them into the units your application uses for tracking.)

Note that non-ranging figures harmonize with small capitals, while ranging figures harmonize with capitals.

Composition details: spacing

Documents set on desktop publishing software often announce their origin because conventions of typewriter style are used which are not normal in professionally typeset matter. Key items are styles for word spacing and punctuation.

In typewriter style, double spacing is still used after punctuation that ends a sentence. This has not been good style for typeset text for over 50 years, and should be avoided. Single spaces only should be the rule. If an extra space is required, as in the example on the right, an en-space should be used, not a double word space.

Paragraph indents should not be created by using word spaces: two en-spaces can be used to create the em-indent which is commonest in text composition, though often inadequate when columns are wide. Alternatively, create the indent using a defined paragraph format. When ragged setting is being used, indents can be abandoned in favour of extra space between paragraphs, as in this book. It does not look professional to combine inter-paragraph spacing *and* indentation.

Composition details: punctuation

Desktop computers have general-purpose keyboards, whereas dedicated typesetting systems include extra keys for certain characters. This means that many dtp users are unaware of the punctuation characters that typesetters use, because they are not visible on the keyboard.

1 **Analysing design**

2 **Learning from experience**

3 **Implementing good design**

An en-space separates the section number from the title better than a single (or double) word space.

There are three distinct characters which are often keyed as the hyphen: the true hyphen, the *en-rule*, and the *em-rule*. The hyphen is the only one with its own key on a computer keyboard; the others are produced by depressing a combination of keys (your manual should explain which). Both the en-rule and the em-rule can be used as a dash (*see below*); the en-rule is also used to show a span of figures (1939–45), between two places to indicate a link (the London–Brighton line), or between two names (Bush–Yeltsin talks). Hyphens look inadequate in these cases. The en-rule will preserve alignment in tabular matter, because it is the same width as the figures.

Quotation marks should never be set as the undifferentiated inch and foot marks which exist on computer keyboards. All PostScript and TrueType typefaces have professional curly, or 'smart', quotes, and these should be used. The closing quote mark should also be used for the *apostrophe*. Some applications will let you key inch marks and substitute the correct characters for you.

Typesetting – good professional typesetting – is perfectly possible with dtp equipment.

Typesetting—good professional typesetting—is perfectly possible with dtp equipment.

Typesetting, 'good professional typesetting', is perfectly possible with dtp equipment.

'Typesetting, "good professional typesetting", is perfectly possible with dtp equipment.'

1991–2
Mason–Dixon line
Mr Lloyd-Jones

The en-rule used between extents of figures (*top*), and between two names (*middle*), to avoid confusion with the hyphen of a single double-barrelled name.

Tom's 1' 6" ruler

Use true apostrophes, not foot marks.

Choose between the *spaced en-rule* for dashes – the style used in this book – and the *unspaced em-rule* (*second example*). Em-rules are designed to join when set side by side, and so can have the effect of joining words rather than separating phrases.

In British style, *single quotes* should be used, reserving *double quotes* to indicate a quote within a quote. Double quotes are more frequently used in the US.

6

How do I choose a typeface?

Typefaces have distinct historical connotations. A study of designs from the fifteenth to the twentieth century shows that they reflect the intellectual and artistic flavour of the period of their creation, as well as technical developments in type-founding and printing. From the fifteenth to the early nineteenth century there was only 'contemporary' typography: style and fashions changed from period to period and from country to country, but because the book was the only significant typographic form developments were gradual and applied across the whole range of printed matter.

Ad lectorem linguæ
GALLICAE STVDIOSVM.

L   Ibros Galeni de vſu partium corpo-
ris humani quum ad Græcum exem
plar magna cura præcipuóque ſtudio non modo recognouiſſem , ſed
propemodū nouos reddidiſſem , vigi
liis , curis, labore fractus, materiā diſquiſiui, in qua
ingenii vires longiore ſtudio & grauiore feſſas re-
crearem , atque reficerem . Cui ọtio nulla mihi
aptior ſeges viſa eſt hac ipſa ſermonis Gallici in-
uentione 'imul ac traditione . Quas res duas dum
ańxie parturio , ańimi contentione non minori
opus mihi eſſe experior , tantæ molis erat linguæ
Gallicæ rationem inuenire ,& in canones coniice-
re. Victa verò tandem operis difficultate , velut in
portum quendam quietiſſimum appulſus mihi
ipſe videor , dum mei laboris fructum non me-
diocrem fore video , ex magna etiam doctorū ex-
pectatione.
Abſoluta igitur vtcunque inſtituti mei parte priori,
quam Iſagøgen in Gallicum ſermonem paraui,
operæpretium me facturum putaui , ſi eam incō-
munem omnium aut vtilitatem aut iucūditatem

a . iiii.

AVIS

AUX SOUSCRIPTEURS

DE

LA GERUSALEMME

LIBERATA

IMPRIMÉE PAR DIDOT L'AÎNÉ

SOUS LA PROTECTION ET PAR LES ORDRES

DE MONSIEUR.

LES ARTISTES choisis par MONSIEUR pour exécuter son édition de LA GERUSALEMME LIBERATA deman-dent avec confiance aux souscripteurs de cet ou-vrage un délai de quelques mois pour en mettre au jour la premiere livraison. Il est rarement arrivé qu'un ouvrage où sont entrés les ornemens de la gravure ait pu être donné au temps préfix pour le-quel il avoit été promis : cet art entraine beaucoup de difficultés qui causent des retards forcés ; et cer-tainement on peut regarder comme un empêche-ment insurmontable les jours courts et obscurs d'un hiver long et rigoureux. D'ailleurs la quantité d'ouvrages de gravure proposés actuellement par

(*Far left*) A possible Garamond typeface used by Robert Esti-enne, Paris, from 1531.

(*Left*) F. A. Didot, a prospectus, 1784: 'the first Modern face'. Such typefaces depended on improvements in presses and paper in order to print clearly.

WANTED,

FOR

A FAMILY IN THE COUNTRY,

A SENSIBLE WELL EDUCATED

Steady Woman,

Qualified to Superintend a Family,

OF STRICT MORALS, HEALTHY, AND GOOD HUMOURED,

BUT ABOVE CORRUPTION,

AND

A THOROUGH GOOD COOK

BOTH AS TO

MEAT, PASTRY, PRESERVES, &c.

SHE will have a proper assistant in the kitchen, and every reasonable encouragement given to her from the Family, according to her qualifications and integrity.

☞ Apply to Mrs. Howe, White-Lion St. Asaph; Mrs. Salusbury, at the Bull Inn, Denbigh; Mrs. Turner, Grocer, in Ruthin; and Mrs. Harrison, in Queen Street, Chester.

CHESTER, PRINTED BY J. MONK,

---

3 *Guineas*
REWARD.

WHEREAS

A SHEEP

Of **Mr. Hancock**, of *Ford*, was in the night between the 14th and 15th instant, **STOLEN** from *Horridge Down*, in the parish of *Milverton*. The Person or Persons who shall give such information, as may be the means of apprehending and bringing the Offender or Offenders to Trial and Conviction, will receive the above Reward. **PHILIP HANCOCK.**
FORD, near Wiveliscombe, 16th October 1829.

J. BAKER, PRINTER, WIVELISCOMBE.

In less than 20 years at the beginning of the nineteenth century, the range of typefaces available to the jobbing printer expanded dramatically. The bookish notice (*left*) was printed in 1812 using types by Fry; the 1829 reward (*right*) uses Thorowgood's Fat Face and a bold Egyptian.

Changes came in the first half of the nineteenth century as type-founders responded to printers' needs for stronger display types (including sans serifs) for posters and handbills, and later as fine book printers, particularly William Morris, turned away from current text types to revive and reinterpret historical designs for their own sake. These two developments produced a great explosion of new and revived typefaces, and provided the basis for the remarkable typographic renaissance of the first half of the twentieth century.

The manufacturers of mechanical composition machines, Linotype and Monotype, competed to issue typefaces representative of every period of printing from

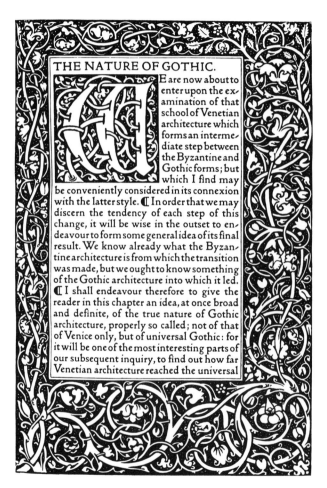

William Morris's Golden type was produced by the innovative technique of photographically enlarging type from fifteenth-century books.

Ransacking the turn-of-the-century type store: an anarchic poster for the last Dada event (1923). Artists of this period regarded typography as a means of free expression.

the fifteenth century, and commissioned excellent new designs. Typography was at the same time deeply influenced by the modern movement in architecture and design, resulting in the German 'new typography' and the influential Bauhaus style. The development of the twentieth-century sans serif has largely been determined by the need to produce typefaces suitable for modern asymmetric design.

A second explosion has followed the establishment of the standard outline font formats such as PostScript. Most are naturally reinterpretations of existing designs, but there are a number of true innovations. Perhaps the most innovative, such as those which mimic screen bitmaps, or exploit PostScript programming to change character shapes over a period of time, are the least likely to be used for book, newspaper, or information design.

Seriffed or sans serif?

This is the question that troubles would-be typographers more than any other. At the height of the modern movement, seriffed typefaces seemed, for good or ill, to represent the cultural traditions of book typography, while sans serifs were promoted as the mode of expression of the modern world – or were vilified as unreadable. Much has happened since to mellow these positions.

It is true that traditional seriffed typefaces are rarely unsuitable for continuous reading, and that few sans serifs are appropriate for this purpose. (Interestingly, it is those sans serifs whose rhythms and spacing relate closely to those of seriffed typefaces that seem most satisfactory for continuous text.) In aesthetic terms, the ideal

Jan Tschichold refined the German 'new typography' to a state of near-perfection. (Prospectus, 1928.)

How do I choose a typeface?

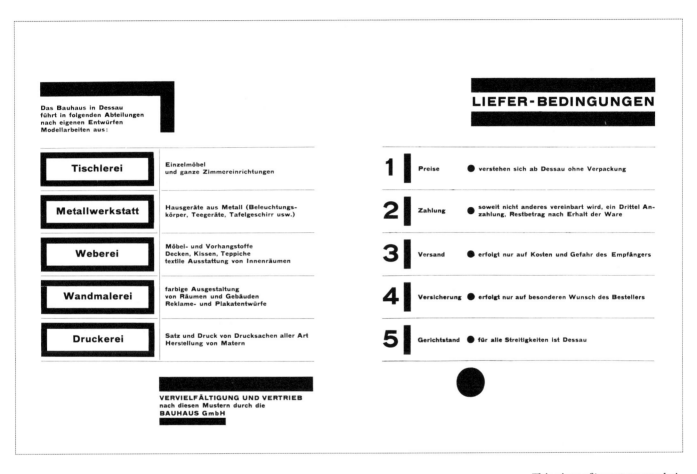

This piece of 'new typography' from the 1920s exploits the sans serif's ability to work with bullets, rules, and other graphic elements to divide the text into accessible chunks, instead of a piece of continuous prose.

RGS RGS

RGS RGS

Good design is always practical design. And what is seen as good type design is, partly, its excellent practical fitness to perform its work. It has a 'heft' and balance in all of its parts just right for its size, as any good tool has. (Neue Helvetica 55)

Good design is always practical design. And what is seen as good type design is, partly, its excellent practical fitness to perform its work. It has a 'heft' and balance in all of its parts just right for its size, as any good tool has. (Frutiger 55)

typeface for continuous prose can be described as one that is just interesting enough to impart some flavour without making itself the focus of the design, and therefore calling attention to itself rather than to the text. This criterion can be applied to both seriffed and sans serif typefaces. The essence of this position is that 'if a typeface is worth looking at, it is worth avoiding'.

But continuous text matter, especially book text, is just one part of today's typography: sans serifs are often most successful when they are at their utmost, exploiting their scope for extreme weight, compactness, and tightness of spacing. In display, these sans serifs make their seriffed equivalents look fussy or anaemic.

With such a variety of typefaces on offer, it is unlikely that you will be able to choose just one that will serve every purpose: typefaces are designed to be different, to do different jobs. It is also unwise to rely on tradition and fix on a typeface whose origins lie in a particular period, hoping that it will be successful for your purposes without testing its suitability more objectively.

Analogies can be drawn between the Regularized Industrial Grotesques and Modern seriffed typefaces, and between Humanist sans serifs and Old Face romans. The examples compare Neue Helvetica with Scotch Roman (*top left*), and Frutiger with Bembo (*above left*). ('Heft' in the text means weight.)

Readability at a given size

Typefaces can be divided into those suitable for very small sizes of text for reference, such as directories and dictionaries, those suitable for continuous reading in books and other documents, and those intended for advertising display, which are either decorative or highly individual. These divisions cut across the historical and structural categories discussed in chapter 3.

Apart from the difference between obviously plain and obviously fancy typefaces, the main feature which determines whether a typeface is suitable for small text composition, normal composition, or display is the strength of drawing. This is strongest in faces for small text composition, lightest in those for display. A block of text for continuous reading set in a typeface with light stroke weights and finely drawn serifs will appear flimsy in comparison with a typeface with heavier letter forms and stubbier serifs. Conversely, a large display headline will look clumsy and loosely spaced when set in a more strongly drawn typeface.

Among conventional serif typefaces of any period, those with a large x-height relative to k–p height will be suitable for small text, those with a small x-height will be suitable for display. This rule does not apply so strictly to sans serif typefaces, because most have a relatively large x-height. It is this feature that makes sans serifs so useful in both very large sizes and very small sizes where clarity is important, e.g. on road signs and in telephone directories.

Legible type

At the present state of affairs there is no scientific answer to the question, What kind of type is most legible? Such reports as come out of the laboratories are not helpful. There is, however, a rough and ready rule for getting some light on this matter – the assumption, namely, that types that have continued in use for a long term of years are legible.

Typefaces used at larger sizes can afford to have more refined character shapes than those used for text composition, where robustness is important. Compare Linotype Caslon 540 used for a heading and Linotype Excelsior used for text (*above*) with the same typefaces reversed (*above right*).

Legible type

At the present state of affairs there is no scientific answer to the question, What kind of type is most legible? Such reports as come out of the laboratories are not helpful. There is, however, a rough and ready rule for getting some light on this matter – the assumption, namely, that types that have continued in use for a long term of years are legible.

How do I choose a typeface?

Good design is always practical design. And what is seen as good type design is, partly, its excellent practical fitness to perform its work. It has a 'heft' and balance in all of its parts just right for its size, as any good tool has.

Ehrhardt in narrow columns.

Good design is always practical design. And what is seen as good type design is, partly, its excellent practical fitness to perform its work. It has a 'heft' and balance in all of its parts just right for its size, as any good tool has. Your letter (if a good artist made it) will have, besides good looks, a suitability to the nth degree to be stamped on paper and read.

Century Schoolbook in a wide column.

Economy of space

Typefaces where the characters are relatively narrow will be more economical of space than those which are wider. Selecting a narrow typeface will be useful in multi-column work – most typefaces designed for newspaper composition are relatively narrow. It is not wise to use a narrow typeface across wide columns: the number of characters in a line will make it more likely that the reader will get lost.

Typefaces which are described as condensed or narrow are usually extremely narrow, and should be used only in very narrow columns, for a few words in a large size of type, or to provide extreme contrast to a typeface of normal width. Condensed typefaces also tend to have emphatic verticals (because horizontal or oblique strokes are reduced in length), which becomes tiring in anything but the narrowest columns.

It is a false economy to choose typefaces with small x-heights for use at small sizes, as this will cram in characters at the expense of readability.

In 1928, **W. A. Dwiggins** wrote that 'there is . . . a rough and ready rule . . . namely, that types that have continued in use for a long term of years are legible. By this test you get a number that you can be sure of – **Scotch Roman,** for example, and the various members of the **Caslon** family.' Dwiggins was writing before the introduction of **Times New Roman,** and many of the Linotype **'legibility group'** typefaces.

This setting in Times shows Univers Condensed used for emphasis.

Monotype Perpetua (*right*) and Times New Roman (*far right*) have similar serif structures and both can be regarded as sharpened-up Old Face romans. But their x-heights are quite different, as these comparative settings at 10/12 pt show.

Units, symbols, and abbreviations

Always use SI units unless there is a good reason for not doing so. If other units are used, please put the SI equivalent in parentheses or provide a conversion table.

Apart from those that are very commonly used, all abbreviated words should be given in full when you first use them, with the abbrevation in parentheses. Decide whether or not you intend to abbreviate and then stick to your decision throughout.

Units, symbols, and abbreviations

Always use SI units unless there is a good reason for not doing so. If other units are used, please put the SI equivalent in parentheses or provide a conversion table.

Apart from those that are very commonly used, all abbreviated words should be given in full when you first use them, with the abbrevation in parentheses. Decide whether or not you intend to abbreviate and then stick to your decision throughout.

When set to matching x–heights, serif typefaces with oblique shading and traditional proportions (Monotype Bembo, Linotype Stempel Garamond) are less economical than designs with vertical shading and a large appearing size (Linotype Centennial, Monotype Nimrod). But typefaces which combine oblique shading with narrow letter forms and large x-heights (Hell Swift, Linotype Olympian, Monotype News Plantin, Monotype Times New Roman) can appear wider than designs of the same width with vertical shading (Linotype Corona, Linotype Centennial, Monotype Nimrod). This gives these typefaces a twofold advantage: they do not suffer from insistent vertical stress, which tends to reduce the differences between the shapes of individual letters, and the eye is carried along the line more effectively by the optical illusion of greater width.

(The text of this book is set in one of these twentieth-century Old Faces, Hell Swift Light 10/12.5 pt, with captions in Hell Swift 8.5/10.5 pt.)

murder
murder

Linotype Centennial (*top*), compared with Times Ten, showing how the oblique shading of Times makes it appear wider.

Character availability

Although PostScript and True-Type fonts have a common character set (see chapter 2), some typeface families are larger than others.

As well as providing a variety of weights of the Latin alphabet, the Monotype Times New Roman typeface family includes Greek, Cyrillic (Russian), and phonetic character sets. If your text requires words or characters from these alphabets, choosing Times New Roman will mean that all the setting will harmonize.

Harmony may or may not be desirable: a series of instructions in English, French, Greek, and Russian would benefit from being set in fonts of the same typeface family. An individual word in Greek in an English text may well be better set in a font that does not harmonize, if this helps the reader to pick out the foreign word.

The Greek alphabet consists of twenty-four letters – seventeen consonants and seven vowels, α, ε,η, ι, ο, υ, ω. In Greek γ may be divided at the end of a line from a following κ or χ. Greek ξ and Latin x between vowels should be taken over, as in δεί-ξειν, proximus, subject to the overriding rule that compound words are divided into their parts.

The Greek alphabet consists of twenty-four letters – seventeen consonants and seven vowels, *α, ε, η, ι, ο, υ, ω.* In Greek *γ* may be divided at the end of a line from a following *κ* or *χ.* Greek *ξ* and Latin *x* between vowels should be taken over, as in *δεί-ξειν, proximus,* subject to the overriding rule that compound words are divided into their parts.

Adobe Lucida has a series of maths extension fonts which enable a variety of mathematical characters to be set which match the characteristics of the basic typeface. The alternative is to use fonts such as Adobe Symbol and Linotype Universal Greek with Math Pi (*pi* is the printer's term for a character that is not part of the normal alphanumeric character set).

Whether individual characters from these non-related fonts match the rest of your setting in weight and apparent size is a matter of chance. They are designed to work with Times and Helvetica, which are strongly drawn and have large x-heights: they do not combine happily with lighter, small x-height faces such as Monotype Garamond (*left*).

Omit the rule (known as the vinculum) from the square root sign. The form √2 is sufficient. *Garamond*

Omit the rule (known as the vinculum) from the square root sign. The form √2 is sufficient. *Times*

This is Ehrhardt, which has an expert set
Thursday 27 August 1992

This is Swift, which has a small capitals font
Thursday 27 August 1992

This is Neue Helvetica 55, with electronically
generated small caps
Thursday 27 August 1992

Fonts within a typeface

If you want to use true small capitals and old style figures with a seriffed typeface, your choice will be restricted to typefaces which have a related expert set (or collection), or a separate small capitals font. Sans serif typefaces are not designed with true small capitals or old style figures. These characters have to be treated as a change of font unless your application includes a routine which can substitute them automatically.

Individual characters

Some typefaces include as part of their normal alphabets characters which are quirkily drawn or easily confused: you should be aware of these if your text is likely to use these characters regularly.

In Monotype Garamond Italic the *h* can be confused with *b*.

In ITC Bookman the Q is excessively quirky.

In Monotype Bembo the long-tailed R can be disturbing, especially in all-cap lines, but an alternative is available in the expert set.

Monotype Bembo and Plantin both have 5-pointed stars instead of conventional asterisks: Baskerville asterisks can be satisfactorily substituted.

(1 Ill)

In Monotype Gill Sans the figure 1 is indistinguishable out of context from capital I and lower case l: use the alternative fonts with a distinctive 1.

Monotype Van Dijck is an accurate historical revival, but is too light for many uses. Monotype Apollo, designed to withstand degradation by photomechanical composition systems, is a sturdier typeface.

Van Dijck

Apollo

Meridien
Meridien
Meridien
Meridien
Meridien
Meridien

Monotype Plantin was designed as a dark typeface to print on glossy art paper, which does not provide much ink squash to thicken the letter forms. It has become a successful face for offset lithography. Linotype Olympian has similarly heavy letters.

Plantin

Olympian

Robustness and resolution of output

Typefaces of the letterpress era were designed to thicken up on reproduction: ink would spread on impact with the paper. This ink squash (or spread) does not occur when digital typefaces are output at high resolution and printed by offset lithography. Seriffed typefaces based on historical examples can look anaemic unless they have been carefully reweighted to take this loss of thickening into account.

Typefaces designed since the advent of photomechanical composition rarely suffer from this defect: these include Monotype Apollo and Linotype Olympian. The latter is a very heavy typeface designed in the 1970s to stand up to photomechanical newspaper composition and high speed rotary letterpress printing.

Robustness is not just a matter of overall weight: Linotype Meridien Medium is a dark typeface, but has extremely fine, tapered serifs which in small sizes can easily disappear. Most sans serif typefaces are relatively robust because they lack the fine line weights and tapering strokes of seriffed typefaces.

The general robustness of a typeface is less important when final output is at high resolution and printing and paper quality can be controlled: it needs to be taken into account when output will be at low resolution, or when final printing and paper quality cannot be guaranteed.

Typefaces designed for low resolution

These should not be confused with bitmap fonts, such as Chicago and Geneva, which are intended for screen displays and produce jagged character forms when printed at any resolution. Typefaces specially designed for 300 dpi output are characterized by even stroke weight, strong serifs, large x-heights, and plain character forms. Intercharacter spacing is generous. Transitions from main stroke to serif, or main stroke to curve, are often abrupt, not modelled, and features which are traditionally rounded (such as the beak of the a) may be squared off.

Adobe Lucida, ITC Officina, and Bitstream Charter share these characteristics, as does Hell Swift, designed as a high-resolution typeface with features to withstand newspaper printing processes. Lucida and Officina have sans serif as well as seriffed variants, which can be used for setting heading or subsidiary text.

Adobe Lucida

abcdefghijklmnopqrstuvwxyz[äöüßåøæœç]
ABCDEFGHIJKLMNOPQRSTUVWXYZ
1234567890(.,:?!$&-*){ÄÖÜÅØÆŒÇ}

ITC Officina and Officina Sans

abcdefghijklmnopqrstuvwxyz[äöüßåøæœç]
ABCDEFGHIJKLMNOPQRSTUVWXYZ
1234567890(.,:?!$&-*){ÄÖÜÅØÆŒÇ}

abcdefghijklmnopqrstuvwxyz[äöüßåøæœç]
ABCDEFGHIJKLMNOPQRSTUVWXYZ
1234567890(.,:?!$&-*){ÄÖÜÅØÆŒÇ}

Bitstream Charter

abcdefghijklmnopqrstuvwxyz[äöüßåøæœç]
ABCDEFGHIJKLMNOPQRSTUVWXYZ
1234567890(.,:?!$&-*){ÄÖÜÅØÆŒÇ}

Typeface choice can help re-inforce or reduce this shift in formality. As with most aspects of typographic design, the effect is cumulative, and greatest when a number of variables work together.

To convey an informal message consider using an informal typeface (especially those designed for low resolution, those with softer letterforms such as Stone Informal, the plainer seriffed typefaces, and some of the Industrial Grotesques). Combined with a simple asymmetric layout, and minimum changes of size or font (*left*), this will look less portentous than a design carried out in a refined seriffed typeface in a centred layout with complex size relationships and heavy use of capitals.

The Bartholomew Players present

Toad of Toad Hall

by A. A. Milne
based on 'The Wind in the Willows'

Tuesday 5 May
Wednesday 6 May

7.30 pm
Bartholomew School, Eynsham

Tickets on sale at Janty's News

THE BARTHOLOMEW PLAYERS

present

TOAD OF TOAD HALL

by A. A. MILNE

based on *The Wind in the Willows*

★

Tuesday 5 & Wednesday 6 May 1992

at the BARTHOLOMEW SCHOOL, *Eynsham*

7.30 *p.m.*

★

Tickets on sale at Janty's News

Formality

The explosion of desktop publishing has meant that documents formerly handwritten or typewritten are now composed using real typefaces. One of the effects of the transition of a document from handwritten or typewritten to typeset form is that it appears to gain in formality and authority. This is appropriate for a book or newspaper, but may make a small-circulation newsletter or announcement look pretentious. If the language used is colloquial or chatty, it will jar when a formal typographic style is used.

Unity and diversity: mixing typefaces

Typewritten text allows little variation or inflexion: one size of type, with only capitals or underscore for emphasis. It is a real danger that the sudden liberation that dtp offers from this straitjacket can lead to a confusing variety of typefaces and styles within a document.

Complex typography works best when it articulates content, rather than drawing attention to its own variety. Typographic variation should be determined by the reader's need to differentiate items of information. Sometimes (usually) this differentiation can be minimal: the occasional word set in italic or small capitals. This will be satisfactory if the speed of reading is slow, the level of concentration high, and the nuance expressed subtle. Differences can be reinforced by adding changes of size, weights, and typeface if the number of text elements to be articulated grows. Remember that changing font or typeface may not be necessary if spacing or indentation can do the job. A principle to follow is that differences should be minimal enough to preserve the overall unity of the page, but provide sufficient variation to be individually identified.

Minimal differences often do not appear as differences at all unless a document is being read through line by line. In a novel the occasional word in italic or capitals can be startling: no further variation of size or typeface need be added. When the reader is scanning the page for information, it is better if more than one variable changes to ensure that the difference is registered: hence combining changes of weight or size with indentation, or changing weight and typeface. This 'belt and braces' approach is called *redundancy* in a design.

References

References should be collated at the end of the chapter or book. Please use one of the following two systems:

1 **The Harvard system** In the text the reference is given as 'Martin (1990)' or '(Martin, 1990)', depending on the context, and the references are listed alphabetically at the end of the text.

2 **The Vancouver system** The references are numbered in their order of appearance in the text, using arabic numerals within square brackets, e.g. '[6]'. In the reference list, the references should be listed in the same numerical sequence.

A satisfactory combination of very bold sans serif headings with a seriffed text (Neue Helvetica 85 and Nimrod). For less successful combinations (Garamond bold with Neue Helvetica 55, *top*; Futura with Nimrod, *bottom*), see the next page.

It is important that these variations do not interfere with the clarity of the text when read word by word, as well as when being scanned. A family of sans serif typefaces (particularly Univers, Frutiger, and some Grotesques) will provide a wider variety of related weights than most seriffed typeface families. Moreover, the linear qualities of sans serifs make their letter forms more easily adaptable to increased weight, whereas very bold seriffed typefaces can look clogged or coarse.

A particularly successful combination of typefaces is to use a seriffed typeface for text with a bold sans serif for headings (see the example on the previous page). This capitalizes on the strengths of the two letter forms: the clarity and compactness of the sans serif, and the easy readability that seriffed type, with strong horizontal flow, gives to continuous text. The combinations to be avoided are generally lighter sans serif headings with dark seriffed text, or using bold (or particularly fussy) seriffed headings with a sans serif text: both can easily look unbalanced.

45 **65** 55 **75** 55 **85**

Weights of Neue Helvetica

Mixing weights within a typeface family, seriffed or sans serif, can be very successful if adjoining weights are avoided in text of similar size: making a bold two weights bolder (or a light two weights lighter) adds the necessary redundancy to ensure that the reader will note the distinction (and improves the tonal contrast of the page).

References

References should be collated at the end of the chapter or book. Please use one of the following two systems:

1 **The Harvard system** In the text the reference is given as 'Martin (1990)' or '(Martin, 1990)', depending on the context, and the references are listed alphabetically at the end of the text.

2 **The Vancouver system** The references are numbered in their order of appearance in the text, using arabic numerals within square brackets, e.g. '[6]'. In the reference list, the references should be listed in the same numerical sequence.

References

References should be collated at the end of the chapter or book. Please use one of the following two systems:

1 The Harvard system In the text the reference is given as 'Martin (1990)' or '(Martin, 1990)', depending on the context, and the references are listed alphabetically at the end of the text.

2 The Vancouver system The references are numbered in their order of appearance in the text, using arabic numerals within square brackets, e.g. '[6]'. In the reference list, the references should be listed in the same numerical sequence.

Mixing two different seriffed or sans serif typefaces calls for considerable skill and is rarely successful unless there is a considerable size (and sometimes weight) difference between the two typefaces – in fact, when the typefaces are being chosen on grounds of optical scaling, with the larger typeface being more detailed, the smaller being sturdier. Both typefaces should normally share the same structural characteristics, although a typeface such as Times New Roman is a neutral enough text face to mate with both Old Face and Modern display types. A considerable difference of weight (which somehow makes an extra bold seriffed type an honorary sans serif) can also make combinations easier.

Headings

Ideally you should use no more than three levels of subheading. If you are writing a single chapter, omit the chapter number.

Units and symbols

Always use SI units unless there is good reason for not doing so.

Swift bold condensed is strong enough to provide headings for Frutiger 55.

READERS'LETTERS

READERS'LETTERS

READERS'LETTERS

Sans serif combinations can also be jarring if a pure Humanist design such as Gill Sans is mated with a Geometrical sans or an Industrial Grotesque: most sans serif families have enough variants to make these couplings unnecessary.

From top: Bureau Grotesque 37 with Gill Sans (not satisfactory); Futura extra bold with Futura light; Franklin Gothic heavy with Frankin Gothic book (much better).

Making informed choices

Typeface choice in the end comes down to continuous experimentation and refinement. Explore the possibilities of typefaces, perhaps choosing a particular group of related typefaces on objective or practical grounds, but then experimenting with individual typefaces within the group to see how the best visual effect can be achieved. Typefaces are subtle: try to become attuned to combinations that work and those that jar. Do not be afraid if you find yourself using a restricted range of typefaces: variety is not the essence of typography, appropriateness for purpose is; and many experienced typographers use a relatively restricted range of typefaces, which they learn to use expertly. Above all, enjoy type. You will be amazed at the pleasure which handling type with a view to its aesthetic and practical aspects can bring.

Part II

Using typefaces

Selecting type for desktop publishing

This section will help guide you through the wide range of typefaces that are available on dtp systems. It will help you identify typefaces and indicate appropriate uses for each one.

Typefaces are divided into seriffed (pp. 91–115) and sans serif designs (pp. 116–123). Within these divisions, typefaces are grouped by style or by well-known names.

The first groups discussed in both seriffed and sans serif categories are those which are available on every dtp system: Times and Helvetica. The strengths and limitations of these basic typefaces are discussed, and the pages which follow are aimed at opening up the range of possible alternatives for different uses.

All the examples are typeset at high resolution, so that design characteristics can be seen easily. Those which are particularly suitable for low-resolution output are noted. To identify a typeface mentioned in the text of this book, turn to the typeface listing (pp. 127–32).

The less experienced user of typefaces needs guidance on which kind of typeface to choose for certain categories of job. While it is impossible to be dogmatic about relating a typeface to a particular use, the following points should be considered:

Decide whether you will print at high or low resolution

Decide whether the document should look formal or informal

Decide how many variant fonts (italic, bold, etc.) are needed

Check whether there is any requirement for particular characters or fonts which may only be available in certain typefaces

If you are printing at low resolution, or producing correspondence, business documentation, etc., consider the sturdier seriffed typefaces (pp. 98–103), informal typefaces (pp. 104–6), and basic sans serifs (pp. 116–21). These will also be suitable for documents which must be photocopied or faxed.

For newsletters and similar multi-column documents, look first at newspaper typefaces (pp. 107–9). For headlines consider the Grotesques and Gothics, especially the condensed ones (pp. 119–21).

If you are preparing a document with a complex range of headings, look at typefaces which have a variety of weights (such as the sans serifs, pp. 116–21). Consider combining these with text set in the plainer seriffed faces, or lighter, wider sans serif faces.

Some typefaces are very refined, e.g. the classic book typefaces (pp. 110–15): they

are shown here to encourage use when high-quality output is available, but also to show that they may not provide satisfactory results at low resolution, or if the document is not intended for formal publication.

Remember to look also for the details of a typeface, which after all finally determine its suitability for a particular purpose. Consider whether figures are clear and even for tabular matter. Consider if punctuation is the right weight (it should be sturdy for small sizes, unobtrusive for large display). Check that the type can withstand reversing out of black, if that is needed. If you have to set across a wide column, do not choose a condensed typeface, and make sure that line spacing is as generous as possible. The short pieces of sample text on the following pages vary in formality and complexity. You will need to assess which typefaces speak in the right 'tone of voice' for the text you are setting.

Finally, remember that simplicity and economy of style are far more useful in typography than indiscriminate use of a variety of styles. Start with one typeface, or one seriffed text face with one sans serif heading face. Be as sparing as you can of the number of times you vary size and weight, but when you do vary these, do it positively. Nothing is worse than a muffled emphasis. If the visual presentation feels at one with the message, your choices of type will have been successful.

Times

beER
beER

Times is probably the most widely used seriffed typeface in the world. Thought of as a universal typeface, it was in fact designed in 1932 for a specific purpose: setting the text of *The Times* of London. As a newspaper typeface, it was designed for the high-quality presswork of *The Times*: few other newspapers could do its brilliance and fine hairlines justice.

Because it combined economy of space with a sharpness of cut unusual in newspaper typefaces, Times gained a reputation as a versatile book composition typeface, and many special characters were produced, as well as Russian and Greek alphabets. It became universal when characters for mathematical setting became available in Times: the typeface travelled well, and was adopted widely in the USA (though less so in Europe).

For dtp use, especially at low resolution, the typefaces shown on pp. 98–103 are more versatile than Times.

minimum illness
minimum illness

▲ The extra weight of Times Bold is taken from the white spaces within the characters. The serif angle is horizontal instead of oblique. These two features make Times Bold look crowded, because they minimize the differences between letters and reduce the apparent space between them.

▶ To avoid the illegibility of Times Bold, consider using Monotype Times Semibold, which follows the roman letter forms more closely. If it does not prove black enough, use a bold sans serif such as Univers or Helvetica (see pp. 116–18), or a bold Egyptian such as Serifa bold (*shown lower right*). (10/12 pt)

▲ In Monotype Times Bold some character widths are actually narrower than in Times New Roman. The oblique stress of the regular font is replaced by the vertical stress of Times Bold. Characters such as b and E change considerably. In Times New Roman, note the spur-less b, the high bar to the e, the long central bar of the E, and the straight tail of the R.

New tyre tread rules

From 1 January 1992 the minimum tyre tread depth must be 1.6 mm for cars, light vans, and their trailers. This depth applies to the central three-quarters of the tread width. **It is an offence to use a vehicle with less than the minimum tread depth.**

New tyre tread rules

From 1 January 1992 the minimum tyre tread depth must be 1.6 mm for cars, light vans, and their trailers. This depth applies to the central three-quarters of the tread width. **It is an offence to use a vehicle with less than the minimum tread depth.**

▶ The extremely large x-height of Times Small Text is 59 per cent of the k–p height.

The appearance of a newspaper has to be governed by both practical and aesthetic considerations. It ought to be pleasing to the eye. It should be so clear as to make the reader's task enjoyable. It should be in accordance with the general style and personality of the newspaper. And the design ought to be appropriate for the methods of production in use at the time.

Silk stockings

In 1599, Henry II of France was the first person to wear silk stockings in that country, at the marriage of his sister.

Queen Elizabeth I, in 1561, was presented with a pair of black silk stockings by her silk-woman, Mrs Montague, and "thenceforth never wore cloth ones any more".

Times Small Text 5.5/7 pt

The appearance of a newspaper has to be governed by both practical and aesthetic considerations. It ought to be pleasing to the eye. It should be so clear as to make the reader's task enjoyable. It should be in accordance with the general style and personality of the newspaper. And the design ought to be appropriate for the methods of production in use at the time.

Silk stockings

In 1599, Henry II of France was the first person to wear silk stockings in that country, at the marriage of his sister.

Queen Elizabeth I, in 1561, was presented with a pair of black silk stockings by her silk-woman, Mrs Montague, and "thenceforth never wore cloth ones any more".

Computer bugs

The first computer bug was just that – a moth which got caught between the relays and stopped the early Harvard Mark II computer in 1946.

Adobe Times 6/7 pt

The appearance of a newspaper has to be governed by both practical and aesthetic considerations. It ought to be pleasing to the eye. It should be so clear as to make the reader's task enjoyable. It should be in accordance with the general style and personality of the newspaper. And the design ought to be appropriate for the methods of production in use at the time.

Silk stockings

In 1599, Henry II of France was the first person to wear silk stockings in that country, at the marriage of his sister.

Queen Elizabeth I, in 1561, was presented with a pair of black silk stockings by her silk-woman, Mrs Montague, and "thenceforth never wore cloth ones any more".

Linotype Olympian 6/8 pt

◀ Because of its origin as a newspaper typeface, Times has been adapted for small sizes. The **Monotype Times Small Text** version is really too extreme for all but the smallest sizes, but if text has to be packed in it performs far better than normal versions. An alternative is to substitute one of the more strongly drawn newspaper faces discussed on pp. 107–9, e.g. **Linotype Olympian.**

▶ Times is still at its best as a high-class magazine typeface, or in technical publications where the wide range of special characters is useful. It is not a satisfactory performer at low resolution, or if reproduction quality is not of the highest: its finesse gone, a rather dull page results. **Monotype Times New Roman** is the original version of the typeface. Using the old style figures and small capitals from the expert set, and allowing generous leading, makes the most of this sharply defined typeface.

S TATELY, plump Buck Mulligan came from the stairhead, bearing a bowl of lather on which a mirror and a razor lay crossed. A yellow dressinggown, ungirdled, was sustained gently behind him by the mild morning air. He held the bowl aloft and intoned:

— *Introibo ad altare Dei.*

Halted, he peered down the dark winding stairs and called up coarsely:

—Come up, Kinch. Come up, you fearful Jesuit.

Solemnly he came forward and mounted the round gunrest. He faced about and blessed gravely thrice the tower, the surrounding country and the awakening mountains. Then, catching sight of Stephen Dedalus, he bent towards him and made rapid crosses in the air, gurgling in his throat

► The hybrid nature of Times, half-way between a newspaper face and a book face, is shown by these comparisons of x-height and serif weight. In x-height, Times is a compromise between the styles, but note that Times has serifs which are lighter and sharper than a bookish typeface such as Adobe Garamond. (*from left*: Monotype Nimrod, Linotype Times Ten, and Adobe Garamond, all 72 pt)

hy hy hy

I remember him as if it were yesterday, as he came plodding to the inn door, his sea-chest following behind him in a hand barrow; a tall, strong, heavy, nut-brown man; his tarry pigtail falling over the shoulders of his soiled blue coat; his hands ragged and scarred, with black, broken nails; and the sabre cut across one cheek, a dirty, livid white. *I remember him looking round the cove and whistling to himself as he did so, and then breaking out in that old sea-song that he sang so often afterwards.*

► Several typefaces designed in the 1950s and 1960s took their cue from Times. **Linotype Life** (*upper*) and **Linotype Concorde** are well-drawn alternatives, which provide similar economy and overall colour, without being quite so 'obvious' as Times. (*Both examples*: 10/12.5 pt)

◄ **Linotype Times Ten** is a useful version for composition at 6–12 pt: at larger sizes it can look heavy. (11/14 pt)

▼ **Adobe Times** (the default on all PostScript devices) is based on the 18 pt Linotype version: it is crowded at text sizes. All versions of Times suffer from capitals that are too large for the lower case.

I remember him as if it were yesterday, as he came plodding to the inn door, his sea-chest following behind him in a hand-barrow; a tall, strong, heavy, nut-brown man; his tarry pigtail falling over the shoulders of his soiled blue coat; his hands ragged and scarred, with black, broken nails; and the sabre cut across one cheek, a dirty, livid white. *I remember him looking round the cove and whistling to himself as he did so, and then breaking out in that old sea-song that he sang so often afterwards.*

I remember him as if it were yesterday, as he came plodding to the inn door, his sea-chest following behind him in a hand-barrow; a tall, strong, heavy, nut-brown man; his tarry pigtail falling over the shoulders of his soiled blue coat; his hands ragged and scarred, with black, broken nails; and the sabre cut across one cheek, a dirty, livid white. *I remember him looking round the cove and whistling to himself as he did so, and then breaking out in that old sea-song that he sang so often afterwards.*

Eel Pie Gravy

Palatino

latin

latin

▲ Palatino in its PostScript version (*top*) compared with the original metal version. The x-height is now larger and curves are less subtle.

Palatino has undergone many transformations since its introduction in 1950. Its latest incarnation, as one of the 'LaserWriter 35', may not be the most elegant, but it is certainly the most widespread. Palatino has been transformed from a rarefied book typeface for fine printing into a more workaday design.

Typefaces such as Palatino are frequently misused, simply because they are so widely available. It was the only typeface in the original 'LaserWriter 35' suitable for text composition that had 'artistic' overtones, and it was therefore pressed into service as a substitute for the wider range of classic book faces.

If you are thinking of using Palatino, ask yourself whether it is really right for the job: considering other typefaces may lead to more enterprising choices. Documents with several weights of heading may require a typeface with stronger bold fonts; at low resolution Palatino italic can look fussy.

Stately, plump Buck Mulligan came from the stairhead, bearing a bowl of lather on which a mirror and a razor lay crossed. A yellow dressinggown, ungirdled, was sustained gently behind him by the mild morning air. He held the bowl aloft and intoned:

— *Introibo ad altare Dei.*

Halted, he peered down the dark winding stairs and called up coarsely:

—Come up, Kinch. Come up, you fearful Jesuit.

▲ Originally designed with a small x-height and long ascenders, Palatino was redrawn by Linotype for photocomposition and emerged as a sturdier typeface with an open x-height and stubby ascenders. The calligraphic italic was retained, but certain quirks of the original, such as the curvature of the S and the serif-less spur of the E, were removed. (12/15 pt)

▶ Palatino was rendered useful for short takes of text in small composition sizes (the example is 8/10 pt), but was compromised for display work.

▼ Palatino italic (*top*) bounces rather oddly along the baseline compared with Photina italic.

magnificent

magnificent

Preparing your typescript

Spacing in copy The copy must be *double-spaced*, and there should be generous margins, especially on the left-hand side.

Contents page There should be a contents page, preferably with page numbers, which makes it easy to locate sections of the text.

Foreign languages If you are quoting books and articles in languages which you do not know thoroughly, it is a good idea to indicate that a copy-editor familiar with these languages should if possible be used.

Headings You should think carefully about the structure of your document – its division into *parts*, *chapters*, and major and minor *sections*.

Photina   Utopia
Photina   **Utopia**
Photina   Utopia
Photina   **Utopia**

▶ **Monotype Photina** (*right*) and **Adobe Utopia** (*far right*) are certainly candidates to rival Palatino as typefaces for formal use. Photina is more sharply drawn than Palatino: it has a cursive and dynamic italic. Utopia has a larger x-height. In PostScript format, both typefaces offer a wider range of weights. (*Upper examples*: 10/13 pt, *lower examples*: 8/10 pt)

Stately, plump Buck Mulligan came from the stairhead, bearing a bowl of lather on which a mirror and a razor lay crossed. A yellow dressinggown, ungirdled, was sustained gently behind him by the mild morning air. He held the bowl aloft and intoned:
— *Introibo ad altare Dei.*
Halted, he peered down the dark winding stairs and called up coarsely:
— Come up, Kinch. Come up, you fearful Jesuit.

Preparing your typescript

Spacing in copy   The copy must be *double-spaced*, and there should be generous margins, especially on the left-hand side.

Contents page   There should be a contents page, preferably with page numbers, which makes it easy to locate sections of the text.

Stately, plump Buck Mulligan came from the stairhead, bearing a bowl of lather on which a mirror and a razor lay crossed. A yellow dressinggown, ungirdled, was sustained gently behind him by the mild morning air. He held the bowl aloft and intoned:
— *Introibo ad altare Dei.*
Halted, he peered down the dark winding stairs and called up coarsely:

Preparing your typescript

Spacing in copy   The copy must be *double-spaced*, and there should be generous margins, especially on the left-hand side.

Contents page   There should be a contents page, preferably with page numbers, which makes it easy to locate sections of

STATELY, plump Buck Mulligan came from the stairhead, bearing a bowl of lather on which a mirror and a razor lay crossed. A yellow dressinggown, ungirdled, was sustained gently behind him by the mild morning air. He held the bowl aloft and intoned:
— *Introibo ad altare Dei.*
Halted, he peered down the dark winding stairs and called up coarsely:

◀ As an alternative for text that needs to look refined but not fussy, **FontFont Scala** is excellent. It has sharply cut serifs, an almost monoline quality, and an interesting italic. (10/13 pt)

▼ If a fully informal typeface is required, consider **ITC Stone Serif**. (10/13 pt)

The Village Toddlers' Playgroup

Treasurer's report for 1991/2

We started the year with a healthy balance of **£206.09**. Our total income in the year was **£2600.06**, and expenditure was **£2262.68**, leaving a balance at year end of **£543.47**.

There is still **£81.25** in outstanding fees owed to us.

ERM

◀ If you need a heavy face in the Palatino mould, **ITC Mendoza** bold is even stronger than Palatino bold – and has touches such as the splayed M and serif-less spur to the E that are more individual. See p. 106 for the book weight which is suitable for informal use.

Bodoni

Typefaces based on the designs of Giambattista Bodoni (1740–1818) appear in all type manufacturers' catalogues. Because they mostly feature extreme vertical stress and considerable contrast between thick and thin styles, they are more valued as examples of virtuoso letter design than as useful typefaces for text composition. The criticism levelled against them at their inception, that they dazzle the reader, is as valid now as it was then: they are not recommended for desktop publishing output at low resolution. Generous line spacing is essential for these typefaces.

▶ If you must use a Bodoni, do use the right one for the circumstances. **Linotype Bauer Bodoni** is an elegant display typeface, with very fine thin strokes: it seems to embody the playfulness of the original Bodoni types better than the more anodyne alternatives. It becomes precious and flimsy at small sizes.

▶ **Monotype Bodoni Book** (*shown here*) and **Linotype Bodoni Book** are true to their name, and the most suitable for text composition, though at 11–13 pt rather than 8–9 pt. Monotype Bodoni and Linotype Bodoni are bland, over-regularized typefaces, which are dazzling in text composition and plain in display. (12/17 pt)

◀ Linotype Bauer Bodoni bold italic.

'Je ne veux que du *magnifique* et je ne travaille pas pour *le vulgaire*.'

GIAMBATTISTA BODONI

I MET a traveller from an antique land
Who said: Two vast and trunkless legs of stone
Stand in the desert . . . Near them, on the sand,
Half sunk, a shattered visage lies, whose frown,
And wrinkled lip, and sneer of cold command,
Tell that its sculptor well those passions read
Which yet survive, stamped on those lifeless things,
The hand that mocked them, and the heart that fed:
And on the pedestal these words appear:
'*My name is Ozymandias, king of kings:*
Look on my works, ye Mighty, and despair!'
Nothing beside remains. Round the decay
Of that colossal wreck, boundless and bare
The lone and level sands stretch far away.

I met a traveller from an antique land
Who said: Two vast and trunkless legs of stone
Stand in the desert . . . Near them, on the sand,
Half sunk, a shattered visage lies, whose frown,
And wrinkled lip, and sneer of cold command,
Tell that its sculptor well those passions read
Which yet survive, stamped on those lifeless things,
The hand that mocked them, and the heart that fed:
And on the pedestal these words appear:
'My name is Ozymandias, king of kings:
Look on my works, ye Mighty, and despair!'
Nothing beside remains. Round the decay
Of that colossal wreck, boundless and bare
The lone and level sands stretch far away.

▲ A regularized Modern with some of the characteristics of the Bodoni typefaces but which avoids extremes can be substituted. This is **Linotype New Caledonia.** (11/15 pt)

▼ **Monotype Walbaum** is shown here in bold. The roman font has a very small appearing size. The Linotype typeface with the same name differs substantially. (12.5/14 pt)

I MET a traveller from an antique land
Who said: Two vast and trunkless legs of stone
Stand in the desert . . . Near them, on the sand,
Half sunk, a shattered visage lies, whose frown,
And wrinkled lip, and sneer of cold command,
Tell that its sculptor well those passions read
Which yet survive, stamped on those lifeless things,
The hand that mocked them, and the heart that fed:
And on the pedestal these words appear:
'My name is Ozymandias, king of kings:
Look on my works, ye Mighty, and despair!'
Nothing beside remains. Round the decay
Of that colossal wreck, boundless and bare
The lone and level sands stretch far away.

ART 1992

▲ The most exciting versions of Bodoni are undoubtedly the very bold variants. They owe less to the designs of Bodoni himself and more to the English Fat Faces of the early nineteenth century. These were extreme versions of Modern typefaces, with great power and dynamism designed for use at very large sizes. **Linotype Bodoni Poster, Monotype Bodoni Ultra Bold** (*shown above*), and **Monotype Falstaff** are examples of this style.

RR

▲ Linotype Bauer Bodoni and Monotype Bodoni compared at 120 pt.

Century Schoolbook

Century Schoolbook is another typeface in the 'LaserWriter 35'. This is **ITC New Century Schoolbook**. Unfortunately several characters are out of balance with each other (o too narrow, e too wide) and the x-height is larger than necessary. Both the **Monotype** and **Bitstream** versions are superior, giving more even character spacing and better horizontal flow. **Century Old Style** is not satisfactory as a text typeface, because it has several quirky characters, and an insistent vertical stress.

An Edwardian printer's views on punctuation

'A working knowledge of punctuation is not to be acquired merely by learning rules; the understanding of an author's meaning should be the earliest study. Next comes a knowledge of the elements of grammar. Careful reading of the standard editions of good authors is always helpful. The compositor should make his own rules, but he cannot do this until he can discriminate the various parts of a sentence.'

An Edwardian printer's views on punctuation

'A working knowledge of punctuation is not to be acquired merely by learning rules; the understanding of an author's meaning should be the earliest study. Next comes a knowledge of the elements of grammar. Careful reading of the standard editions of good authors is always helpful. The compositor should make his own rules, but he cannot do this until he can discriminate the various parts of a sentence.'

◀ ITC Century Schoolbook. (10/12.5 pt)

◀ Monotype Century Schoolbook has a smaller x-height, and wider characters. (10/12.5 pt)

Regale Regale Regale

◀ Century Schoolbook (*bottom*) is a development of the nineteenth-century Modern group of typefaces, exemplified here by Monotype Modern Extended (*top left*). 'Schoolbook' indicates that it is a variation of the original Century typeface, which was similar to Linotype Century Expanded (*top right*).

Century Schoolbook, Amasis, and Clarion are particularly versatile for technical and business documentation, because they are plain and combine well with bold (and bold sans serif) headings. These faces, with generous line spacing, work well over wide columns. Note how the typefaces with stronger serifs survive better when reversed white out of black.

An Edwardian printer's views on punctuation

'A working knowledge of punctuation is not to be acquired merely by learning rules; the understanding of an author's meaning should be the earliest study. Next comes a knowledge of the elements of grammar. Careful reading of the standard editions of good authors is always helpful. The compositor should make his own rules, but he cannot do this until he can discriminate the various parts of a sentence.'

◄ For use at low resolution, consider **Monotype Amasis**, which is a slab-serif typeface (a descendant of the nineteenth-century Egyptians). It is very sturdy at small sizes, yet more economical of space than other faces designed for low-resolution output. (10/12.5 pt)

An Edwardian printer's views on punctuation

CRafg

CRafg

CRafg

CRafg

CRafg

'A working knowledge of punctuation is not to be acquired merely by learning rules; the understanding of an author's meaning should be the earliest study. Next comes a knowledge of the elements of grammar. Careful reading of the standard editions of good authors is always helpful. The compositor should make his own rules, but he cannot do this until he can discriminate the various parts of a sentence.'

◄ For text composition where less rather than more individuality is an advantage, for example newspaper text, **Monotype Clarion** (very similar to Nimrod) provides an even larger x-height and better space economy, and very good rendering at low resolution. (9/12.5 pt)

An Edwardian printer's views on punctuation

'A working knowledge of punctuation is not to be acquired merely by learning rules; the understanding of an author's meaning should be the earliest study. Next comes a knowledge of the elements of grammar. Careful reading of the standard editions of good authors is always helpful. The compositor should make his own rules, but he cannot do this until he can discriminate the various parts of a sentence.'

◄ For larger sizes of composition, or display, **Linotype New Caledonia** is a truly elegant typeface, with a logical range of weights. Its disadvantages are that it can look fussy in small sizes, and does not reproduce well at low resolution, where its subtleties are lost. (10.5/13pt)

▲ (*From top*) New Century Schoolbook, Century Old Style, Amasis, Clarion, and New Caledonia.

Versatile seriffed typefaces

Plantin, and typefaces with similar heftiness, are more suited to low-resolution output than Times, and should be considered for dtp text composition of lengthy reports, newsletters, etc. (For correspondence, the faces on pp. 104–6 are more suitable.)

▶ **Monotype Plantin** was designed in 1913 with a particular purpose in mind: as a heavily drawn typeface to withstand the thinning effects of letterpress printing on art paper, which made traditionally weighted typefaces look weak. It was originally a slightly condensed typeface, but the digital version of Plantin was based on the broad 8 pt metal drawings, so it has a comfortable 'spread' as well as plenty of colour. (12/15 pt)

New tyre tread rules

From 1 January 1992 the minimum tyre tread depth must be 1.6 mm for cars, light vans, and their trailers. This depth applies to the central three-quarters of the tread width.

It is an offence to use a vehicle with less than the minimum tread depth.

▲ Plantin's asterisk is a five-pointed star.

▲ Plantin (*top*) was probably the model for Times New Roman, which can be regarded as a skilful sharpening-up of the older typeface.

bgsAMPW,;''
bgsAMPW,;''
bgsAMPW,;

Flight times from Paris

▲ Plantin is also excellent for reversing out of a solid colour, as its blunt serifs do not fill in easily.

▲ *From top to bottom*: Plantin, Plantin italic, Plantin bold. Earmark characters: b without foot serif, s with serifs on inside only; A with blunt top serif, splayed M, open-bowl P, crossed W. Punctuation marks are prominent and very clear, even when small.

Williamsburg News Plantin

Williamsburg Plantin

Williamsburg News Plantin bold

Williamsburg Plantin bold

Williamsburg Plantin light

Williamsburg Plantin semibold

Chapter One

I REMEMBER him as if it were yesterday, as he came plodding to the inn door, his sea-chest following behind him in a hand-barrow; a tall strong, heavy, nut-brown man; his tarry pigtail falling over the shoulders of his soiled blue coat; his hands ragged and scarred, with black, broken nails; and the sabre cut across one cheek, a dirty, livid white. *I remember him looking round the cove and whistling to himself as he did so, and then breaking out in that old sea-song that he sang so often afterwards.*

Preparing your typescript

Spacing in copy   The copy must be *double-spaced*, and there should be generous margins, especially on the left-hand side.

Contents page   There should be a contents page, preferably with page numbers, which makes it easy to locate sections of the text.

Foreign languages   If you are quoting books and articles in languages which you do not know thoroughly, it is a good idea to indicate that a copy-editor familiar with these languages should if possible be used.

Headings   You should think carefully about the structure of your document – its division into *parts*, *chapters*, and major and minor *sections*. Within chapters the hierarchy of *sections*, *subsections*, *sub-subsections*, etc. should be clear: it helps if the different headings are typed in a different way.

◀ Plantin in 8/10 pt (*left*) showing subheadings picked out in the excellent bold.

▲ Plantin in 13/17 pt (*above*) showing its strong horizontal flow. Plantin italic, which is almost as wide as the roman, performs well in text sizes to differentiate individual words. It is not elegant in display.

Of the alternatives to Plantin, **Hell Swift** is by far the best as an all-purpose dtp typeface. Designed for newspaper production in the 1980s, it is excellent at surviving low-resolution output and newspaper and newsletter production standards. It has a dynamic, contemporary feel, emphasized by the sharpness with which curves and straight lines join. It gives, with Plantin, a strong horizontal flow which seems to pull the reader's eye effortlessly along the line: this is due to its carefully balanced oblique stress. Sharply defined details such as serifs and the beak of the g do not break down under less than perfect conditions. The text of this book is set in Swift Light, with captions in the regular weight.

Hell Hollander is a more refined version of Swift designed for use at larger sizes: Swift's angles are transformed into curves, and abrupt junctions between straight and curved strokes are softened. Hollander is a perfect display face to work with Swift text.

▶ 9.5/11 pt Swift for text used with 22/24 pt Hollander bold.

▼ Swift and italic (*top*), Hollander and italic (*bottom*).

fast

fast

fast

fast

Swift bold   **Plantin bold**

Choosing the right typeface

A newspaper *must* be printed at high speed; the paper it is printed on *must* be of a certain kind. In the designing of the newspaper itself, and in the designing of typefaces for it, these practical limitations *must* take precedence over aesthetic consideration.

What seemed to be needed for modern newspaper work was a type in which the profiles of the letters are so clear in the original state that they can survive the destructive effect of production and still present a crisp appearance at the end.

Preparing your typescript

Spacing in copy   The copy must be *double-spaced*, and there should be generous margins, especially on the left-hand side.

Contents page   There should be a contents page, preferably with page numbers, which makes it easy to locate sections of the text.

Foreign languages   If you are quoting books and articles in languages which you do not know thoroughly, it is a good idea to indicate that a copy-editor familiar with these languages should if possible be used.

Preparing your typescript

Spacing in copy   The copy must be *double-spaced*, and there should be generous margins, especially on the left-hand side.

Contents page   There should be a contents page, preferably with page numbers, which makes it easy to locate sections of the text.

Foreign languages   If you are quoting books and articles in languages which you do not know thoroughly, it is a good idea to indicate that a copy-editor familiar with these languages should if possible be used.

▲ Swift bold is not as strong as Plantin bold. A sans serif bold such as Frutiger black can provide the necessary weight.

Linotype Trump Mediaeval is a quirkier typeface than either Plantin or Swift, but also provides a good, dense page that does not suffer from thinning down when printed. Trump punctuation can seem obtrusive, however, as commas and quotation marks consist of calligraphic 'flicks' rather than the more conventional rounded forms.

The italic is an unusual one, being less condensed and cursive than most seriffed italics. It belongs to a group known as 'sloped romans', where the upright letter forms are redrawn on the slant, with some modification, to provide the italic. This approach should be distinguished from electronically sloped italic, when the character is simply slanted without modification, resulting in a distorted appearance. Trump is one of the more successful sloped romans, because critical characters – *a*, *e*, and *f* – have true italic forms.

Minimum official conditions
Minimum official conditions

Minimum official conditions
Minimum official conditions
Minimum official conditions

▲ Trump Mediaeval and italic (*top*), showing how a sloped roman occupies as much space as a roman, while a true italic (Hollander) is narrower. The bottom line shows Hollander electronically sloped.

fn

fn

I remember him as if it were yesterday, as he came plodding to the inn door, his sea-chest following behind him in a hand-barrow; a tall strong, heavy, nut-brown man; his tarry pigtail falling over the shoulders of his soiled blue coat; his hands ragged and scarred, with black, broken nails; and the sabre cut across one cheek, a dirty, livid white. *I remember him looking round the cove and whistling to himself as he did so, and then breaking out in that old sea-song that he sang so often afterwards.*

▲ Trump has a greater vertical stress than Plantin, and characters combine less closely into words. (12/15 pt)

◀ The bold is less wide than Plantin bold, and the considerable space between characters dilutes the blackness of the typeface.

Trump Mediaeval bold Plantin bold

Informal and low-resolution typefaces

The arrival of desktop publishing and the laser printer has led to the development of a number of 'informal' typefaces. You should use these when a document needs to have more legibility than an apparently typewritten one, but would look overdesigned in a traditional book typeface. They are designed to print at low resolution and to withstand faxing and photocopying.

A particular use for these typefaces is for correspondence, or corporate documentation which may be produced within a company on dtp equipment. Typefaces which simply imitate typewriters, even to the extent of giving each character the same width, are an anachronism. But there is much to be said for the absolute neutrality of a typewriter, the fact that the reader perceives it to be without the 'tone of voice' that any more sophisticated typeface possesses. Several of the typefaces discussed here have both seriffed and sans serif forms, allowing them to be used for both text (seriffed) and headings (sans serif).

▶ **ITC Officina** is modelled on typewriter antecedents, resembling the style known as Letter Gothic. It achieves the neutrality of typewriting without the stilted letter forms.

The seriffed and sans serif versions of this typeface can be used on their own, or together. The example shows the serriffed version of Officina with the sans serif used for bold headings. Using seriffed headings with sans serif text is less satisfactory. (10.5/12.5 pt)

agy
agy

Officina Sans and **bold**
Officina Serif and **bold**

To   Paul

From   Ruth

Subject **Redrawing screen bitmap characters**

I'd hoped to get the enclosed to you at the end of last week, but we needed more time to print them all out. Here is a summary of the points we discussed:

1   Anglo-Saxon characters

You redesigned 7 characters at the 12 pt screen bitmap size, and I attach printouts. You offered to cast your eye over the same characters at the 14, 18, and 24 pt screen bitmap sizes.

2   Other characters

The page symbol and pointing hand are less important, but I have added them to the printouts.

I need all the characters by the end of the month (for phase 2 beta-testing), but two weeks later would be acceptable if you are very busy. Please let me know now if this sounds reasonable.

Thanks in advance!

FAX

To	**Stuart**	Subject	**PC fonts**
From	**Paul**	Date	**23 January**

Thanks for arranging for the correct-format disks to be sent to Aylesbury. I was very impressed by the service you gave on this, and I'm sure that the project is now back on schedule.

Do keep me posted on any new services you offer connected with desktop publishing.

abs
abs

◀ **Adobe Lucida** was planned from the outset with low resolution in mind, hence the wide character spacing and stubby serifs which resist degradation. There is a companion sans serif. (10/12.5 pt)

▶ **ITC Stone Informal** perhaps plays the 'informal' style rather too much – rounding of the character shapes and serifs looks fine in laser printer output, but looks merely 'cute' at high resolution.

▶ **ITC Stone Serif** (*right*) is a more subtle typeface, which can successfully replace a bookish one such as Palatino in many circumstances.

ITC Stone Sans (*far right*) can be used in the same ways as Officina Sans, on its own, or as a companion bold to the seriffed version.

The library will reopen on Tuesday 15 April

Will all readers please note that in future **no bags or umbrellas** will be allowed on the premises

Typesetting systems, especially desktop typesetting systems, *should* be put in the hands of designers. Not because a designer has an aesthetic sensibility to arrange display type, or to choose a striking typeface, but because designers should be the guardians of readability.

If the designer is elevated from specifier to implementer, he may realize how much care craftsmen of the past put into their work, and be inspired to

Typesetting systems, especially desktop typesetting systems, *should* be put in the hands of designers. Not because a designer has an aesthetic sensibility to arrange display type, or to choose a striking typeface, but because designers should be the guardians of readability.

If the designer is elevated from specifier to implementer, he may realize how much care craftsmen of the past put into their work, and be inspired to do the same.

Selecting type for desktop publishing

- Decide whether you will print at high or low resolution

- Decide whether the document should look formal or informal

- Decide how many variant fonts (italic, bold, etc.) are needed

- Check whether there are any requirements for particular characters or fonts which may only be available in certain typefaces

Selecting type for desktop publishing

- Decide whether you will print at high or low resolution

- Decide whether the document should look formal or informal

- Decide how many variant fonts (italic, bold, etc.) are needed

- Check whether there are any requirements for particular characters or fonts which may only be available in certain typefaces

afg

◀ **Bitstream Charter** (*above and upper example left*) avoids breaking up at 300 dpi by the radical method of using only the most basic shapes from which to build characters. Serifs and terminals are reduced to straight lines, but with such care that a spare and elegant typeface results. **Monotype Amasis** (*below and lower example left*) produces a slightly softer, more condensed effect. Both typefaces reverse out of black well. (*Both examples*: 11/15 pt)

afg

▶ **ITC Mendoza** (*right*, 14/18.5 pt) and **Hell Swift** (*far right*, 12/16 pt) can also be called upon in informal contexts and will perform well.

Dear Angus: I must say that I find the proofs that you sent me last week quite intolerable. However hard I try, I can find nothing to which I can take exception; everything that I have asked for has been taken into account; they are perfect . . . Can you wonder I feel frustrated and ill used?

The Netherlands

It's hard to imagine how a country of clog-wearers, so rigidly loving of the still life and professing **pea soup** as its national dish, could have spawned a craze that was to sweep Europe and turn otherwise sensible citizens into *tulip maniacs*.

Newspaper typefaces

Many of the reproduction problems newspaper typefaces were designed to overcome resemble those of output at low resolution on today's laser printers. Because they were designed to have a deliberately neutral, rather than bookish, appearance, you can use them when more 'artistic' typefaces might call attention to themselves. Like the Lucida, Charter, Officina group of typefaces, they are appropriate for uses when typewriter fonts are unconvincing but traditional book typefaces are over-refined.

Newspaper typography of the interwar period produced one great and several important typefaces. Times New Roman is seen as the pre-eminent English newspaper typeface of the period, but among newspapers it was hardly ever used outside the carefully printed pages of *The Times* itself. US and European newspapers generally used a range of typefaces developed by Linotype and known (unscientifically) as the 'legibility group'.

Note how justified setting across narrow columns leads to erratic word spacing.

▼ Ionic and Excelsior were the earliest members of the 'legibility group'. **Monotype Ionic** has a huge x-height and prominent serifs, and needs considerable leading to be readable in bulk. The bold is too narrow, and should be replaced in display by a bold sans serif. (8/9 pt)

Ionic

Newspaper typography

The appearance of a newspaper has to be governed by both practical and aesthetic considerations. It ought to be pleasing to the eye. It should be so clear as to make the reader's task enjoyable. It should be in accordance with the general style and personality of the newspaper. And the design ought to be appropriate for the methods of production in use at the time.

Silk stockings

In 1599, Henry II of France was the first person to wear silk stockings in that country, at the marriage of his sister.

Queen Elizabeth I, in 1561, was presented with a pair of black silk stockings by her silkwoman, Mrs Montague, and "thenceforth never wore cloth ones any more".

Computer bugs

The first computer bug was just that – a moth which got

▼ **Linotype Excelsior** is more considered, with a lower x-height and stronger horizontal flow. Excelsior bold is not as effective as the roman – a strong weight of a sans serif such as ITC Franklin Gothic provides better contrast. (8/9pt)

Excelsior

Newspaper typography

The appearance of a newspaper has to be governed by both practical and aesthetic considerations. It ought to be pleasing to the eye. It should be so clear as to make the reader's task enjoyable. It should be in accordance with the general style and personality of the newspaper. And the design ought to be appropriate for the methods of production in use at the time.

Silk stockings

In 1599, Henry II of France was the first person to wear silk stockings in that country, at the marriage of his sister.

Queen Elizabeth I, in 1561, was presented with a pair of black silk stockings by her silkwoman, Mrs Montague, and "thenceforth never wore cloth ones any more".

Computer bugs

The first computer bug was just that – a moth which got caught between the relays and stopped the early Harvard Mark II com-

▼ **Linotype Coron**a can be regarded as a stronger version of Century Schoolbook, suitable for use at 8–9 pt. With more widely spaced characters than Excelsior, it can lack horizontal cohesion, and is the least versatile of this group of faces. Nimrod and Olympian (or Century Schoolbook itself) are better choices. (8/9 pt)

▼ **Linotype Olympian** was designed specifically for newspapers using photomechanical composition, and sought to avoid the starkness of Ionic and the condensed feel of Corona. Extremely successful, it has surprisingly subtle design details for so sturdy a face. Like Nimrod, it has a usefulness beyond newspaper typography. The roman and italic perform well at low resolution, but the bold will not appear strong enough: mating with a bold sans serif is recommended. (8/9 pt)

▼ **Monotype Nimrod** is an excellent 'neutral' typeface, drawing on the strengths of the 'legibility group', but taking digital production methods into account. It is better spaced than Corona or Excelsior, and has a good bold and bold italic. Never beautiful, Nimrod always looks efficient for tables and short paragraphs of technical text, and is one of the few typefaces that can genuinely be used (at high resolution) in 5 pt. It should be used with generous line spacing across narrow columns. (8/9 pt)

Corona

Newspaper typography

The appearance of a newspaper has to be governed by both practical and aesthetic considerations. It ought to be pleasing to the eye. It should be so clear as to make the reader's task enjoyable. It should be in accordance with the general style and personality of the newspaper. And the design ought to be appropriate for the methods of production in use at the time.

Silk stockings

In 1599, Henry II of France was the first person to wear silk stockings in that country, at the marriage of his sister.

Queen Elizabeth I, in 1561, was presented with a pair of black silk stockings by her silk-woman, Mrs Montague, and "thenceforth never wore cloth ones any more".

Computer bugs

The first computer bug was just that – a moth which got

Olympian

Newspaper typography

The appearance of a newspaper has to be governed by both practical and aesthetic considerations. It ought to be pleasing to the eye. It should be so clear as to make the reader's task enjoyable. It should be in accordance with the general style and personality of the newspaper. And the design ought to be appropriate for the methods of production in use at the time.

Silk stockings

In 1599, Henry II of France was the first person to wear silk stockings in that country, at the marriage of his sister.

Queen Elizabeth I, in 1561, was presented with a pair of black silk stockings by her silk-woman, Mrs Montague, and "thenceforth never wore cloth ones any more".

Computer bugs

The first computer bug was just that – a moth which got caught between the relays and stopped the early Harvard

Nimrod

Newspaper typography

The appearance of a newspaper has to be governed by both practical and aesthetic considerations. It ought to be pleasing to the eye. It should be so clear as to make the reader's task enjoyable. It should be in accordance with the general style and personality of the newspaper. And the design ought to be appropriate for the methods of production in use at the time.

Silk stockings

In 1599, Henry II of France was the first person to wear silk stockings in that country, at the marriage of his sister.

Queen Elizabeth I, in 1561, was presented with a pair of black silk stockings by her silk-woman, Mrs Montague, and "thenceforth never wore cloth ones any more".

Computer bugs

The first computer bug was just that – a moth which got caught between the relays and stopped the early Harvard

▼ **Linotype Times Ten** is the most serviceable version of Times for narrow newspaper columns. **Bitstream Dutch 801** is almost identical. The most bookish of all newspaper typefaces, Times does not provide such an even column weight as Olympian or Swift. It is more readable for longer articles than Nimrod, which has an insistent vertical stress unless generously leaded. Paragraphs set entirely in Times Bold dazzle the reader. (8/9 pt)

▼ **Monotype News Plantin** is an attempt to provide an alternative to Times which has a sturdy weight and even colour. It has a blander feel in mass than a more sharply drawn face such as Swift. It is even more economical of space than Times and can appear very small on the page. For most dtp uses, Monotype Plantin (p. 100) is a better choice. (8/9 pt)

▼ **Hell Swift** is more satisfactory than News Plantin because of the sharpness of its overall design. Junctions between strokes are more abrupt, and there is a strong horizontal flow, which give a dynamic feel. As with Nimrod and Olympian, Swift is useful for typesetting in small sizes for directories, indexes, tabular matter, etc., as well as newspapers and magazines. (8/9 pt)

Times Ten

Newspaper typography

The appearance of a newspaper has to be governed by both practical and aesthetic considerations. It ought to be pleasing to the eye. It should be so clear as to make the reader's task enjoyable. It should be in accordance with the general style and personality of the newspaper. And the design ought to be appropriate for the methods of production in use at the time.

Silk stockings

In 1599, Henry II of France was the first person to wear silk stockings in that country, at the marriage of his sister.

Queen Elizabeth I, in 1561, was presented with a pair of black silk stockings by her silk-woman, Mrs Montague, and "thenceforth never wore cloth ones any more".

Computer bugs

The first computer bug was just that – a moth which got caught between the relays and stopped the early Harvard Mark II computer in 1946.

News Plantin

Newspaper typography

The appearance of a newspaper has to be governed by both practical and aesthetic considerations. It ought to be pleasing to the eye. It should be so clear as to make the reader's task enjoyable. It should be in accordance with the general style and personality of the newspaper. And the design ought to be appropriate for the methods of production in use at the time.

Silk stockings

In 1599, Henry II of France was the first person to wear silk stockings in that country, at the marriage of his sister.

Queen Elizabeth I, in 1561, was presented with a pair of black silk stockings by her silk-woman, Mrs Montague, and "thenceforth never wore cloth ones any more".

Computer bugs

The first computer bug was just that – a moth which got caught between the relays and stopped the early Harvard Mark II computer in 1946.

Swift

Newspaper typography

The appearance of a newspaper has to be governed by both practical and aesthetic considerations. It ought to be pleasing to the eye. It should be so clear as to make the reader's task enjoyable. It should be in accordance with the general style and personality of the newspaper. And the design ought to be appropriate for the methods of production in use at the time.

Silk stockings

In 1599, Henry II of France was the first person to wear silk stockings in that country, at the marriage of his sister.

Queen Elizabeth I, in 1561, was presented with a pair of black silk stockings by her silk-woman, Mrs Montague, and "thenceforth never wore cloth ones any more".

Computer bugs

The first computer bug was just that – a moth which got caught between the relays and stopped the early Harvard Mark II com-

Classic book typefaces

Classic book typefaces present a dilemma for the typographer today. The designs developed for hot-metal composing machines in the first fifty years of this century constitute one of the great treasures of typographic design. They restored to printers versions of historical designs which are among the most beautiful, and the most readable, typefaces for books (Monotype Bembo, Garamond, and Bell; Linotype Granjon) and proved that new designs could be as pleasing as the old (Linotype Caledonia and Electra; Monotype Dante and Centaur). But all were designed with the constraints, and effect, of letterpress printing in mind. The very care with which they were adapted to machine composition has meant that digital versions often do not measure up to the 'original' metal designs. This is mainly because a single drawing now has to suffice for all possible sizes: metal types were designed with a new drawing for every one or two sizes, enabling a high degree of optical fine tuning to take place in the design.

When quickly
When jobs quickly ma
When jobs quickly mar

▲ Enlargements of metal Bembo characters showing how the design was amended to perform effectively at different sizes:
6 pt (*top*), 8 pt (*middle*) , and 12 pt (*bottom*). At smaller sizes x-heights were large, serifs prominent, and overall the characters were wide and heavy. At larger sizes x-heights were reduced, serifs became smaller and sharper, and overall the characters were narrower and lighter.

The PostScript version of Bembo has been based, realistically and correctly, on one of the sturdier and more open composition sizes. As a result it can look pedestrian in large sizes, where the x-height should be smaller, ascenders and descenders longer.

Bembo
Bembo
Bembo
Bembo
Bembo
Bembo
Bembo
Bembo
BEMBO

▼ **Monotype Bembo** was a prime example of 'optical scaling'. Although it is no longer the book face *par excellence* that its metal forebear was, it is still an effective typeface for composition at text sizes, especially at 12 pt and smaller. (11.75/13.25 pt)

FOOLISHLY, she had set them opposite each other. That could be remedied tomorrow. If it were fine, they should go for a picnic. Everything seemed possible. Everything seemed right. Just now (but this cannot last, she thought, dissociating herself from the moment while they were talking about boots) just now she had reached security; she hovered like a hawk suspended; like a flag floated in an element of joy which filled every nerve of her body fully and sweetly, not noisily, solemnly rather, for it arose, she thought, looking at them all eating there, from husband and children and friends; all of which rising in this profound stillness (she was helping William Bankes to one very small piece more and peered into the depths of the earthenware pot) seemed now for no special reason to stay there like smoke, like a fume rising upwards, holding them safe together. Nothing need be said; nothing could be said. There it was, all around them. It partook, she felt, carefully helping Mr Bankes to a specially tender piece, of eternity; as she had already felt about something different once before that afternoon; there is coherence in things, a stability; something, she meant, is immune from change, and shines out (she glanced at the window with its ripple of reflected lights) in the face of the *flowing, the fleeting, the spectral, like a ruby; so that again tonight she had the feeling she had had once today already, of*

Garamond
Garamond
Garamond
Garamond
Garamond
GARAMOND

▼ **Monotype Garamond** has a more graceful feel than Bembo, but is really too light for many uses. The original italic is very elegant but fussy, with characters which slope erratically and which may be ambiguous in text sizes. The alternative italic (shown here) is more regular, but still narrow. (11.5/13 pt)

Centaur
Centaur
Centaur
Centaur

▼ **Monotype Centaur** provides more effective display sizes than Bembo or Garamond, because it has been revised more radically. It needs to be set at sizes above 12 pt to come into its own, however. It is not recommended for low-resolution output at small sizes. (13/14 pt)

FOOLISHLY, she had set them opposite each other. That could be remedied tomorrow. If it were fine, they should go for a picnic. Everything seemed possible. Everything seemed right. Just now (but this cannot last, she thought, dissociating herself from the moment while they were talking about boots) just now she had reached security; she hovered like a hawk suspended; like a flag floated in an element of joy which filled every nerve of her body fully and sweetly, not noisily, solemnly rather, for it arose, she thought, looking at them all eating there, from husband and children and friends; all of which rising in this profound stillness (she was helping William Bankes to one very small piece more and peered into the depths of the earthenware pot) seemed now for no special reason to stay there like smoke, like a fume rising upwards, holding them safe together. Nothing need be said; nothing could be said. There it was, all around them. It partook, she felt, carefully helping Mr Bankes to a specially tender piece, of eternity; as she had already felt about something different once before that afternoon; there is coherence in things, a stability; something, she meant, is immune from change, and shines out (she glanced at the window with its ripple of reflected lights) in the face of the flowing, the fleeting, the spectral, like a ruby; so that again tonight she had the feeling she had had once today *already, of peace, of rest. Of such moments, she thought, the thing is made that remains for ever after. This would remain.*

Foolishly, she had set them opposite each other. That could be remedied tomorrow. If it were fine, they should go for a picnic. Everything seemed possible. Everything seemed right. Just now (but this cannot last, she thought, dissociating herself from the moment while they were talking about boots) just now she had reached security; she hovered like a hawk suspended; like a flag floated in an element of joy which filled every nerve of her body fully and sweetly, not noisily, solemnly rather, for it arose, she thought, looking at them all eating there, from husband and children and friends; all of which rising in this profound stillness (she was helping William Bankes to one very small piece more and peered into the depths of the earthenware pot) seemed now for no special reason to stay there like smoke, like a fume rising upwards, holding them safe together. Nothing need be said; nothing could be said. There it was, all around them. It partook, she felt, carefully helping Mr Bankes to a specially tender piece, of eternity; as she had already felt about something different once before that afternoon; there is coherence in things, a stability; something, she meant, is immune from change, and shines out (she *glanced at the window with its ripple of reflected lights) in the face of the flowing, the fleeting, the spectral, like a ruby; so that again tonight*

Minion
Minion
Minion
Minion
Minion
Minion
Minion
MINION

If these classics shown on the previous pages fail to live up to expectations, what alternatives can be found?

▼ **Adobe Minion** is one of the best of the new 'classic' designs, which looks elegant in display sizes but has an x-height that is large enough for clarity in text sizes. (11/13.5 pt)

Dante
Dante
Dante
Dante
Dante
Dante

▼ **Monotype Dante** is a recent redesign of a traditionally designed old face, and because it has been adapted with digital output firmly in mind, it is an effective typeface, stronger than Monotype Garamond and better at larger composition sizes than Bembo. (11.5/13.5 pt)

Foolishly, she had set them opposite each other. That could be remedied tomorrow. If it were fine, they should go for a picnic. Everything seemed possible. Everything seemed right. Just now (but this cannot last, she thought, dissociating herself from the moment while they were talking about boots) just now she had reached security; she hovered like a hawk suspended; like a flag floated in an element of joy which filled every nerve of her body fully and sweetly, not noisily, solemnly rather, for it arose, she thought, looking at them all eating there, from husband and children and friends; all of which rising in this profound stillness (she was helping William Bankes to one very small piece more and peered into the depths of the earthenware pot) seemed now for no special reason to stay there like smoke, like a fume rising upwards, holding them safe together. Nothing need be said; nothing could be said. There it was, all around them. It partook, she felt, carefully helping Mr Bankes to a specially tender piece, of eternity; as she had already felt about something different once before that afternoon; there is coherence in things, a stability; something, she meant, is immune from change, and shines out (she glanced at the window with its ripple of reflected lights) in the face of the flowing, the fleeting, the spectral, like a ruby; so that again tonight she had the feel-*ing she had had once today already, of peace, of rest. Of such moments, she thought, the thing is made that remains for*

Foolishly, she had set them opposite each other. That could be remedied tomorrow. If it were fine, they should go for a picnic. Everything seemed possible. Everything seemed right. Just now (but this cannot last, she thought, dissociating herself from the moment while they were talking about boots) just now she had reached security; she hovered like a hawk suspended; like a flag floated in an element of joy which filled every nerve of her body fully and sweetly, not noisily, solemnly rather, for it arose, she thought, looking at them all eating there, from husband and children and friends; all of which rising in this profound stillness (she was helping William Bankes to one very small piece more and peered into the depths of the earthenware pot) seemed now for no special reason to stay there like smoke, like a fume rising upwards, holding them safe together. Nothing need be said; nothing could be said. There it was, all around them. It partook, she felt, carefully helping Mr Bankes to a specially tender piece, of eternity; as she had already felt about something different once before that afternoon; there is coherence in things, a stability; something, she meant, is immune from change, and shines out (she glanced at the window with its ripple of reflected lights) in the face of the flowing, the fleeting, the spectral, like a ruby; so that again tonight she *had the feeling she had had once today already, of peace, of rest. Of such moments, she thought, the thing is made that remains*

Stempel Garamond
Stempel Garamond
Stempel Garamond
Stempel Garamond

▼ **Linotype Stempel Garamond** provides a sturdier classic text face than the Monotype version (Linotype Garamond 3 is not as elegant). Although it has a somewhat vertical stress, emphasized by its tall capitals, Stempel Garamond produces a darker page, and stronger, less cupped serifs make it more resistant to degradation at low resolution. There is a certain looseness in its letter spacing. (10.5/13 pt)

Sabon
Sabon
Sabon
Sabon
Sabon

▼ **Linotype Sabon** shows how the Garamond idiom can be reworked to produce a stronger, more contemporary typeface. The most widely useful typeface in this group, Sabon can provide a more elegant alternative to Times in wide-column setting. The italic is not at all fussy, and performs well in text sizes, less well in display. See p. 50 for a comparison with the Monotype version. (10/13 pt)

Foolishly, she had set them opposite each other. That could be remedied tomorrow. If it were fine, they should go for a picnic. Everything seemed possible. Everything seemed right. Just now (but this cannot last, she thought, dissociating herself from the moment while they were talking about boots) just now she had reached security; she hovered like a hawk suspended; like a flag floated in an element of joy which filled every nerve of her body fully and sweetly, not noisily, solemnly rather, for it arose, she thought, looking at them all eating there, from husband and children and friends; all of which rising in this profound stillness (she was helping William Bankes to one very small piece more and peered into the depths of the earthenware pot) seemed now for no special reason to stay there like smoke, like a fume rising upwards, holding them safe together. Nothing need be said; nothing could be said. There it was, all around them. It partook, she felt, carefully helping Mr Bankes to a specially tender piece, of eternity; as she had already felt about something different once before that afternoon; there is coherence in things, a stability; something, she meant, is immune from change, and shines out (she glanced at the window with its ripple of reflected lights) in the face of the flowing, the fleeting, the spectral, like a ruby; so that again tonight she *had the feeling she had had once today already, of peace, of rest. Of such moments, she thought, the thing is made that remains for ever after. This would remain.*

Foolishly, she had set them opposite each other. That could be remedied tomorrow. If it were fine, they should go for a picnic. Everything seemed possible. Everything seemed right. Just now (but this cannot last, she thought, dissociating herself from the moment while they were talking about boots) just now she had reached security; she hovered like a hawk suspended; like a flag floated in an element of joy which filled every nerve of her body fully and sweetly, not noisily, solemnly rather, for it arose, she thought, looking at them all eating there, from husband and children and friends; all of which rising in this profound stillness (she was helping William Bankes to one very small piece more and peered into the depths of the earthenware pot) seemed now for no special reason to stay there like smoke, like a fume rising upwards, holding them safe together. Nothing need be said; nothing could be said. There it was, all around them. It partook, she felt, carefully helping Mr Bankes to a specially tender piece, of eternity; as she had already felt about something different once before that afternoon; there is coherence in things, a stability; something, she meant, is immune from change, and shines out (she glanced at the window with its ripple of reflected lights) in the face of the flowing, the fleeting, the spectral, like a ruby; so that again tonight she had the feeling she had had once today already, *of peace, of rest. Of such moments, she thought, the thing is made that remains for ever after. This would remain.*

Ehrhardt
Ehrhardt
Ehrhardt
Ehrhardt
EHRHARDT

Janson Text
Janson Text
Janson Text
Janson Text
JANSON TEXT

FOOLISHLY, she had set them opposite each other. That could be remedied tomorrow. If it were fine, they should go for a picnic. Everything seemed possible. Everything seemed right. Just now (but this cannot last, she thought, dissociating herself from the moment while they were talking about boots) just now she had reached security; she hovered like a hawk suspended; like a flag floated in an element of joy which filled every nerve of her body fully and sweetly, not noisily, solemnly rather, for it arose, she thought, looking at them all eating there, from husband and children and friends; all of which rising in this profound stillness (she was helping William Bankes to one very small piece more and peered into the depths of the earthenware pot) seemed now for no special reason to stay there like smoke, like a fume rising upwards, holding them safe together. Nothing need be said; nothing could be said. There it was, all around them. It partook, she felt, carefully helping Mr Bankes to a specially tender piece, of eternity; as she had already felt about something different once before that afternoon; there is coherence in things, a stability; something, she meant, is immune from change, and shines out (she glanced at the window with its ripple of reflected lights) in the face of the flowing, the fleeting, the spectral, like a ruby; so that again tonight she had the feeling she had had once today already, of peace, of rest. *Of such moments, she thought, the thing is made that remains for ever after. This would remain.*

Foolishly, she had set them opposite each other. That could be remedied tomorrow. If it were fine, they should go for a picnic. Everything seemed possible. Everything seemed right. Just now (but this cannot last, she thought, dissociating herself from the moment while they were talking about boots) just now she had reached security; she hovered like a hawk suspended; like a flag floated in an element of joy which filled every nerve of her body fully and sweetly, not noisily, solemnly rather, for it arose, she thought, looking at them all eating there, from husband and children and friends; all of which rising in this profound stillness (she was helping William Bankes to one very small piece more and peered into the depths of the earthenware pot) seemed now for no special reason to stay there like smoke, like a fume rising upwards, holding them safe together. Nothing need be said; nothing could be said. There it was, all around them. It partook, she felt, carefully helping Mr Bankes to a specially tender piece, of eternity; as she had already felt about something different once before that afternoon; there is coherence in things, a stability; something, she meant, is immune from change, and shines out (she glanced at the window with its ripple of reflected lights) in the face of the flowing, the fleeting, the spectral, like a ruby; so that again tonight she had the *feeling she had had once today already, of peace, of rest. Of such moments, she thought, the thing is made that remains for ever*

Baskerville
Baskerville
Baskerville
Baskerville
Baskerville
Baskerville
BASKERVILLE

▼ **Monotype Baskerville** lacks overall weight, although it is a more classically drawn face than ITC New Baskerville. It can look weak at low resolution, and can tend towards blandness. (11/13.5 pt)

Bell
Bell
Bell
Bell

▼ **Monotype Bell** is an alternative eighteenth-century typeface. It has the advantage in PostScript form of a semibold weight, which can replace the normal roman in shortish texts. Bell needs to be seen in generous sizes at high resolution to be appreciated; there are no straight lines at all in the character shapes. (11/13.5 pt)

FOOLISHLY, she had set them opposite each other. That could be remedied tomorrow. If it were fine, they should go for a picnic. Everything seemed possible. Everything seemed right. Just now (but this cannot last, she thought, dissociating herself from the moment while they were talking about boots) just now she had reached security; she hovered like a hawk suspended; like a flag floated in an element of joy which filled every nerve of her body fully and sweetly, not noisily, solemnly rather, for it arose, she thought, looking at them all eating there, from husband and children and friends; all of which rising in this profound stillness (she was helping William Bankes to one very small piece more and peered into the depths of the earthenware pot) seemed now for no special reason to stay there like smoke, like a fume rising upwards, holding them safe together. Nothing need be said; nothing could be said. There it was, all around them. It partook, she felt, carefully helping Mr Bankes to a specially tender piece, of eternity; as she had already felt about something different once before that afternoon; there is coherence in things, a stability; something, she meant, is immune from change, and shines out (she glanced at the window with its ripple of reflected lights) in the face of the flowing, the fleeting, the spectral, like a ruby; so that again tonight she *had the feeling she had had once today already, of peace, of rest. Of such moments, she thought, the thing is made that remains for ever*

Foolishly, she had set them opposite each other. That could be remedied tomorrow. If it were fine, they should go for a picnic. Everything seemed possible. Everything seemed right. Just now (but this cannot last, she thought, dissociating herself from the moment while they were talking about boots) just now she had reached security; she hovered like a hawk suspended; like a flag floated in an element of joy which filled every nerve of her body fully and sweetly, not noisily, solemnly rather, for it arose, she thought, looking at them all eating there, from husband and children and friends; all of which rising in this profound stillness (she was helping William Bankes to one very small piece more and peered into the depths of the earthenware pot) seemed now for no special reason to stay there like smoke, like a fume rising upwards, holding them safe together. Nothing need be said; nothing could be said. There it was, all around them. It partook, she felt, carefully helping Mr Bankes to a specially tender piece, of eternity; as she had already felt about something different once before that afternoon; there is coherence in things, a stability; something, she meant, is immune from change, and shines out (she glanced at the window with its ripple of reflected lights) in the face of the flowing, the fleeting, the spec-*tral, like a ruby; so that again tonight she had the feeling she had had once today already, of peace, of rest. Of such moments,*

Helvetica and Univers

Helvetica is probably the most widely used sans serif typeface at present, offering a huge range of variants for both text composition and display. Designed in 1957, it represents a 'machine aesthetic', being a regularized version of the German industrial sans serifs of the early twentieth century. It became popular because it seemed to represent qualities of modernism to designers influenced by the Swiss modernist movement.

Although it has excellent bolds, which can be used for headings with a variety of seriffed typefaces, Helvetica is less suitable for continuous text.

Helvetica regular and bold

Helvetica light and black

Condensed
Condensed

Compressed
Compressed
Compressed

◀ The default **Adobe Helvetica** resident on all LaserWriters is not ideal: it suffers from crudeness of drawing, especially in the tail of the R and the lower-case a. This is obvious at large sizes. The typeface is cramped when small, because many letters, especially i, l, and t, are insufficiently spaced. Weights other than those supplied as the default are better: the black is particularly strong.

◀ The compressed variants are energetic; the condensed versions tend to be flabby, with soft curves which seem to fight against the narrow character shapes.

Those of the **Constructivists** who sought most consciously to become artist–engineers found the fields of typographical and poster design to be the most fruitful. Here it was possible for the artist to make use of the most modern processes and skills and yet not to reduce the result to the level of the machine – as was inevitable in mass-production where industrialization, even at this point in Russia, demanded standardization. Thus **Rodchenko, Lissitsky, Klutsis,** and **Alexei Gan** worked

Those of the **Constructivists** who sought most consciously to become artist–engineers found the fields of typographical and poster design to be the most fruitful. Here it was possible for the artist to make use of the most modern processes and skills and yet not to reduce the result to the level of the machine – as was inevitable in mass-production where industrialization, even at this point in Russia, demanded standardization. Thus **Rodchenko, Lissitsky, Klutsis,** and **Alexei Gan** worked

◀ **Linotype Neue Helvetica** (shown *left*, compared with Adobe Helvetica *far left*) is a redrawing which has produced a typeface with stronger horizontal flow and a more logical range of weights. It·offers better-fitted display sizes and less jerky text setting, as the letter fit is more even. This is counterbalanced by an increased blandness in text composition, as the typeface has suffered even more regularization than its forebear. (*All text examples*: 9/12.5 pt)

Linotype Univers is a better typeface on most systems than Helvetica, because the character spacing is more open, and words such as 'illegible' do not look so uneven as they do in Helvetica. This is particularly important in text composition. PostScript Univers medium 55 has a strong horizontal flow, and the black 75 provides a better bold contrast than Univers 65. Univers light 45 is better balanced than the equivalent Helvetica font, because the more open spacing of the former emphasizes the rhythm of the thin strokes.

If you wish to move away from Helvetica in text composition, Univers will provide a more legible substitute. Univers can be less satisfactory in display sizes, because it is generally not so closely fitted, and does not have such a comprehensive range of bold, compressed variants.

For text composition, especially across wider columns, all sans serifs need more generous line spacing than seriffed typefaces. Do not allow less than the spacing shown in these examples.

▼ A less mechanical alternative to Helvetica and Univers is the semi-Humanist **Linotype Frutiger**. It has excellent open character spacing which makes it more suitable for setting continuous text.

▼ Univers 55 with black 75. (9/12.5 pt)

Those of the **Constructivists** who sought most consciously to become artist–engineers found the fields of typographical and poster design to be the most fruitful. Here it was possible for the artist to make use of the most modern processes and skills and yet not to reduce the result to the level of the machine – as was inevitable in mass-production where industrialization, even at this point in Russia, demanded standardization. Thus **Rodchenko, Lissitsky, Klutsis,** and

▶ Univers condensed is not satisfactory for continuous text, but the bolder weights are excellent for headings. The character shapes have been condensed more successfully than those of Helvetica.

▼ Univers light 45 with bold 65. (9/12.5 pt)

Those of the **Constructivists** who sought most consciously to become artist–engineers found the fields of typographical and poster design to be the most fruitful. Here it was possible for the artist to make use of the most modern processes and skills and yet not to reduce the result to the level of the machine – as was inevitable in mass-production where industrialization, even at this point in Russia, demanded standardization. Thus **Rodchenko, Lissitsky, Klutsis,** and **Alexei Gan** worked out

Constructivists
Constructivists
Constructivists

Those of the **Constructivists** who sought most consciously to become artist–engineers found the fields of typographical and poster design to be the most fruitful. Here it was possible for the artist to make use of the most modern processes and skills and yet

Those of the **Constructivists** who sought most consciously to become artist–engineers found the fields of typographical and poster design to be the most fruitful. Here it was possible for the artist to make use of the most modern processes and skills and yet not to

◀ **Monotype Arial** has letters drawn to the same widths as Adobe Helvetica, so it can be substituted without affecting the number of words in a line. Because its character shapes are closer to those of the less regularized Grotesques it is more suitable for text composition.

▶ Helvetica light and black	Regulation *Regulation*	**Regulation** ***Regulation***
▶ Helvetica regular and bold	Regulation *Regulation*	**Regulation** ***Regulation***
▶ Neue Helvetica 55 and 75	Regulation *Regulation*	**Regulation** ***Regulation***
▶ Univers 55 and 75	Regulation *Regulation*	**Regulation** ***Regulation***
▶ Frutiger 55 and 75	Regulation *Regulation*	**Regulation** ***Regulation***
▶ Arial regular and bold	Regulation *Regulation*	**Regulation** ***Regulation***

Grotesques and Gothics

Sans serifs are excellent for headings and strong display. If you wish to move away from the Helvetica–Univers style and explore the original Industrial Grotesques (Gothics), the typefaces to consider are **Monotype Grotesque** and **ITC Franklin Gothic. Linotype Akzidenz Grotesk, News Gothic,** and **Font Bureau Grotesque** also fall into this category. Of these, Monotype Grotesque and ITC Franklin Gothic are the most suitable for text composition. Only ITC Franklin Gothic offers a full range of weights and styles for both text composition and display.

▶ **Monotype Grotesque** is excellent for text composition: it has open but regular character spacing and good horizontal flow, but retains sufficient irregularity in character shapes to provide some sparkle on the page. Monotype Grotesque Light is considerably lighter, and lacks a separate semibold. (10/13.5 pt)

aGaGaG
aGaGaG

Those of the **Constructivists** who sought most consciously to become artist–engineers found the fields of typographical and poster design to be the most fruitful. Here it was possible for the artist to make use of the most modern processes and skills and yet not to reduce the result to the level of the machine – as was inevitable in mass-production where industrialization, even at this point in Russia, demanded standard-ization. Thus **Rodchenko, Lissitsky, Klutsis,** and **Alexei Gan** worked out pion-eer examples of modern typographical design.

Those of the **Constructivists** who sought most consciously to become artist–engineers found the fields of typographical and poster design to be the most fruitful. Here it was

◀ Monotype Grotesque (*top*) with equivalent weights of Neue Helvetica. Such an 'unrecon-structed' Grotesque suffers from a disadvantage against the bat-talions of Univers and Helvetica because it does not have a range of carefully graded weights and widths: it is more suitable for occasions when a single weight with just a simple bold or italic variant will suffice. Where more variant fonts are essential, use ITC Franklin Gothic.

▼ **Font Bureau Grotesques** are based on designs by the Stephen-son Blake Foundry from the early part of the century. These type-faces have not had the inconsis-tencies ironed out of them. Suitable only for display.

Grotesque 13
Grotesque 15
Grotesque 17
Grotesque 37
Grotesque 53
Grotesque 79

▶ **ITC Franklin Gothic** is the only Gothic which is available in a wide range of weights, and is therefore the most versatile. It produces good text composition especially in narrow columns, with particularly effective bolds. Because they are very strong, the bold weights can be used (at quite small sizes) as headings in seriffed text. The regular weights can then provide a useful alternative text style for notes, tables, references, and other secondary matter. The character spacing is tight, but this is counterbalanced by the broadness and individuality of the letter forms.

With a larger x-height than Monotype Grotesque, Franklin Gothic has an American rather than European flavour. (10/13.5 pt)

Those of the **Constructivists** who sought most consciously to become artist–engineers found the fields of typographical and poster design to be the most fruitful. Here it was possible for the artist to make use of the most modern processes and skills and yet not to reduce the result to the level of the machine – as was inevitable in mass-production where industrialization, even at this point in Russia, demanded standardization. Thus **Rodchenko, Lissitsky, Klutsis,** and **Alexei Gan** worked out pioneer examples of modern typographical design.

Those of the **Constructivists** who sought most consciously to become artist–engineers found the fields of typographical and poster design to be the most fruitful. Here it was possible for the artist to make use of the most modern processes and skills and yet not to reduce the result to the level of the machine – as was inevitable in mass-production where industrialization, even at this point in Russia, demanded standardization. Thus **Rodchenko, Lissitsky, Klutsis,** and **Alexei Gan** worked out pioneer examples of modern typographical design.

▶ **Linotype ATF Franklin Gothic** (*top*) and **Linotype ATF Franklin Gothic Condensed** provide stronger, tighter display sizes for newsletter headlines than the bolds of ITC Franklin Gothic.

Modern art
Modern art

▲ **Berthold Adzidenz Grotesk** has a distinctly Germanic flavour, and produces elegant text with a surprisingly small x-height. It is rather loosely fitted in display sizes. Annoyingly, there are no italic or bold italic fonts. (10/13.5 pt)

Those of the **Constructivists** who sought most consciously to become artist–engineers found the fields of typographical and poster design to be the most fruitful. Here it was possible for the artist to make use of the most modern processes and skills and yet not to reduce the result to the level of the machine – as was inevitable in mass-production where industrialization, even at this point in Russia, demanded standardization.

Those of the **Constructivists** who sought most consciously to become artist–engineers found the fields of typographical and poster design to be the most fruitful. Here it was possible for the artist to make use of the most modern processes and skills and yet not to reduce the result to the level of the machine – as was inevitable in mass-production where industrialization

◀ **Linotype News Gothic** (*far left*) and **Monotype News Gothic** (*left*) are closer in design to the original metal types than ITC Franklin Gothic, which has been heavily redrawn. Although they have large x-heights, they are less good for continuous text. The Monotype version is very loosely spaced, which can be undesirable. (10/13.5 pt)

▶ Monotype Grotesque Light
(use the bold of the regular
weight; no bold italic)

Regulation
Regulation

▶ Monotype Grotesque regular
and bold (no bold italic)

Regulation
Regulation

Regulation

▶ ITC Franklin Gothic book and
demibold

Regulation
Regulation

Regulation
Regulation

▶ Akzidenz Grotesk regular (no
italic or bold italic)

Regulation

Regulation

▶ Linotype News Gothic regular
and bold

Regulation
Regulation

Regulation
Regulation

▶ Monotype News Gothic regular and bold (no bold italic)

Regulation
Regulation

Regulation

Gill Sans and Futura

▼ **Gill Sans** letter forms are closely related to other seriffed typefaces by the same designer. (*From top*) Gill Sans, Perpetua, Joanna. Note the distinctive g and a.

53 Woodcock Lane, Eynsham, Oxford

....

Location

Turn left from our offices and Woodcock Lane is the third turning on the right. Number 53 faces the children's boating lake.

Description

A newly built detached house with very spacious living rooms, and three bedrooms, all with adjoining bathrooms.

Rooms and fittings

Hall	Staircase to first floor
Cloakroom	WC, basin
Kitchen	12 × 10 ft. Gas cooker
Dining room	16 × 11 ft. Double-glazed patio windows

....

Monotype Gill Sans and **Linotype Futura** have such significance in the development of the twentieth-century sans serif that it is easy to regard them as more useful in everyday typography than they really are. Respectively English (Eric Gill) and German (Paul Renner), they seem to embody the cultures they originated in: Gill Sans is patrician and coldly conservative, Futura is so thorough in its radical reworking of the alphabet that it seems at first glance to be entirely mechanical.

Regular 23
Regular 23
Regular 23

The success of any process of design depends upon a sympathetic attitude on the part of the designer towards the material he undertakes to shape. The material, when its conditions are understood and met, itself meets the designer halfway. *It performs a part of the designing process of its own accord* – suggests modifications, points out which ways to turn. But if its peculiarities are ignored or opposed it retaliates by cancelling out all the good features that the

▲ Gill Sans is heavily influenced by calligrapher Edward Johnston's alphabet (*above*) for the London transport system, drawn in 1919. The Johnston alphabet was not designed for text setting, but for signs and display.

▲ Gill Sans rarely works successfully with other typefaces, whether sans serif or seriffed. Joanna, also designed by Eric Gill, is an exception, because of the underlying similarity of many of the character shapes.

◀ Gill Sans has such a strong personality that it can be difficult to use as a text typeface, where neutrality is an advantage. The italic has cursive forms of *f* and *a* which are rarely found in sans serif faces. (12/16 pt)

▶ **Futura** seems more amenable: it can be made to work with the lighter seriffed typefaces, not with other varieties of sans serif. But Futura's weakness is again in text composition because of the problems that always ensue when the differences between letters are reduced. A page set in Futura presents the reader with too many circles and straight lines, and not enough real *letters* to be read. It reduces text to geometrical patterns, which can be arresting in large sizes but are merely dazzling in continuous text. (14/18 pt)

▶ **ITC Avant Garde** is in the same idiom as Futura, but its massive x-height removes Futura's redeeming quality of elegance.

▶ There are typefaces in the Humanist (neo-Gill) and Geometric (neo-Futura) styles which are easier to use. These include **Linotype Avenir, Frutiger, Syntax,** and **Lucida**. All need generous line spacing.

Avenir is the most geometric design. Frutiger shares characteristics with the regularized Industrial Grotesques such as Univers, and is very versatile. Lucida Sans is an informal typeface. Syntax has a distinct character, which may be too obtrusive for some texts. (*All examples*: 10/13 pt)

The success of any process of design depends upon a sympathetic attitude on the part of the designer towards the material he undertakes to shape. The material, when its conditions are understood and met, itself meets the designer halfway. *It performs a part of the designing process of its own accord* – suggests modifications, points out which ways to

Romantic
Romantic

Ra
bq

▲ On enlargement Futura reveals that apparently monoline circles are carefully thinned when they join a straight stroke.

53 Woodcock Lane

Description
A newly built *detached house* with very spacious living rooms, and three bedrooms, each with adjoining bathroom.

▲ Avenir

▼ Lucida Sans

53 Woodcock Lane

Description
A newly built *detached house* with very spacious living rooms, and three bedrooms, each with adjoining bathroom.

▲ Frutiger

▼ Syntax

53 Woodcock Lane

Description
A newly built *detached house* with very spacious living rooms, and three bedrooms, each with adjoining bathroom.

53 Woodcock Lane

Description
A newly built *detached house* with very spacious living rooms, and three bedrooms, each with adjoining bathroom.

Manufacturers' addresses

The following list gives the UK, US, and European addresses of the major typeface manufacturers. You will find further comments on the manufacturers marked * on pp. 28–30.

Companies have cross-licensing agreements, which means that they can sell typefaces made by another manufacturer: you should make clear when you order that you want a typeface from a particular manufacturer's library.

Manufacturers and their dealers may offer different discounts, and you should check on these. You should also check that the typeface is available in the format (Macintosh or IBM PC, PostScript or TrueType) that is correct for your equipment.

Typefaces are usually sold in volumes, which means a collection of fonts that may or may not constitute the whole of a typeface family. There are also special packs which contain a manufacturer's idea (often curious) of what forms a useful range of typefaces, e.g. for newsletters.

Bitstream and Scangraphic sell individual fonts as well as volumes on floppy disk. Adobe, Agfa, Bitstream, and Monotype also sell entire typeface libraries on compact disc (CD-ROM), or you can buy a CD and unlock individual fonts for a charge.

Telephone numbers for the UK and US are given as national numbers; those for Europe are given as international numbers.

Adobe*

UK
Adobe Systems, 10 Princetown Mews, 167–169 London Road, Kingston-upon-Thames, Middlesex KT2 6PT, UK
tel 081-547 1900
fax 081-547 3515

available from FontWorks UK (*see entry*)

available from P and P Micro plc, Toddhall Road, Carrs Industrial Estate, Haslingdon, Rossendale, Lancashire BB4 5HL, UK
tel (0706) 217744

USA
Adobe Systems Inc., 1585 Charleston Road, PO Box 7900, Mountain View, CA 94039-7900, USA
tel (415) 961-4400

Europe
Adobe Systems Europe BV, Office Centre, Josef Israelskaed 48C, 1072 SB Amsterdam, The Netherlands
tel +31 20 676 7661
fax +31 20 675 4086

Agfa*

USA
Agfa Corporation, 90 Industrial Way, Wilmington, MA 01887, USA
tel (508) 658-5600
fax (508) 657-8268

Europe including UK
Agfa Compugraphic, 88 Industrial Estate, Shannon, Co. Clare, Ireland
tel +353 61 61011
fax +353 61 62702

Manufacturers' addresses

Berthold

Berthold Exclusiv typefaces, a wide range of typefaces suitable for advertising, but less so for text composition, are available in PostScript format from Adobe. Some Berthold typefaces are licensed to and sold by Linotype.

available from Adobe *or* Linotype (*see entries*)

Bitstream

UK
Bitstream International Ltd., 2 Court Mews, London Road, Charlton Kings, Cheltenham, Gloucestershire GL52 6HS, UK
tel (0242) 227377
fax (0242) 251319

USA
Bitstream Inc., Athenaeum House, 215 First Street, Cambridge, MA 02142, USA
tel (617) 497-6222
fax (617) 868-4732

Europe
available from FontWorks Germany (*see entry*)

Elsner & Flake Designstudios

Manufacturer of all ITC typefaces, as well as some Hell faces (including the Swift family used for the composition of this book), and exclusive designs.

UK and USA
available from FontWorks/FontShop (*see entry*)

Europe
Dorfstraße 11, 2081 Langeln, Germany
tel +49 4123 4843
fax +49 4123 6027

Émigré Graphics

Manufacturers of experimental designer typefaces that look like bitmaps (but aren't) – handle with care!

available from FontWorks/FontShop (*see entry*)

Font Bureau

Revivals of unusual typefaces from UK and US foundries.

available from FontWorks/FontShop *and* Monotype (*see entries*)

FontFont

Range of new designer typefaces including the excellent Scala and Meta.

available from FontWorks/FontShop (*see entry*)

FontWorks/FontShop

Distributors for all the manufacturers listed here except Linotype, as well as for Alphabets, Bear Rock, ClubType, EmDash, Electric Typographer, Giampa Textware, ATF/Kingsley, LetterPerfect, MacCampus/Kempgen, TreacyFaces.

UK
FontWorks UK, 65–69 East Road, London N1 6AH, UK
tel 071-490 5390
fax 071-490 5391

North America
FontShop Canada, 401 Wellington Street West, Toronto, Ontario M5V 1E8, Canada
free phone for all North America (800) 36-FONTS
tel (416) 348-9837
fax (416) 593-4318

Europe
FontShop Germany, Bergmannstraße 102, 1000 Berlin 61,
Germany
tel +49 30 69006262
fax +49 30 69006277

Linotype*

UK
Linotype-Hell Ltd., Bath Road, Cheltenham, Gloucestershire
GL53 7LR, UK
tel (0242) 222354
fax (0242) 222357

USA
Linotype-Hell Company, 425 Oser Avenue, Hauppauge,
NY 11788-9890, USA
tel (516) 434-2000
fax (516) 434-2748

Europe
Linotype-Hell AG, Postfach 5660, Mergenthaler Allee 55–75,
6236 Eschborn bei Frankfurt, Germany
tel +49 6196 982

Linguists' Software

Manufacturer of non-Latin typefaces (Hebrew, Greek), not
drawn to high-quality typesetting standards but with good
keyboard layouts, for use in academic foreign-
language setting.

available from FontWorks/FontShop (*see entry*)

Monotype*

UK
Monotype Typography, Salfords, Redhill RH1 5JP, UK
tel (0737) 765959
fax (0737) 769243

USA
Monotype Typography Inc., Suite 504, 53 West Jackson
Boulevard, Chicago, IL 60604, USA
(312) 855-1440
fax (312) 939-0378

Europe
Monotype GmbH, Arnsburger Straße 68–90,
6000 Frankfurt 60, Germany
tel +49 69 4050040
fax +49 69 4960064

Scangraphic

Manufacturer of high-quality advertising display typefaces:
not for the casual dtp user.

UK
Scangraphic Visutek Ltd., Caxton House, Randalls Way,
Leatherhead, Surrey KT22 7TW, UK
tel (0372) 378652
fax (0372) 379420

Europe
Mannesmann Scangraphic GmbH, Rissenerstraße 112–114,
2000 Wedel Hamburg, Germany
tel +49 4103 8010

Typeface listing

Lт Antique Olive
Reg Antique Olive
Iта *Antique Olive*
Bd **Antique Olive**
Blk **Antique Olive**
BdCon **Antique Olive**
Cmp **Antique Olive**
Nrd **Antique Olive**
NrdIta ***Antique Olive***

Lт Akzidenz Grotesk
Reg Akzidenz Grotesk
Bd **Akzidenz Grotesk**
Blk **Akzidenz Grotesk**

Reg Amasis
Iта *Amasis*
Bd **Amasis**
BdIta ***Amasis***

Reg Apollo
Iта *Apollo*
SemBd **Apollo**

Reg Arial
Iта *Arial*
Bd **Arial**
BdIta ***Arial***
Lт Arial
LтIta *Arial*
Blk **Arial**
BlkIta ***Arial***
Med Arial
MedIta *Arial*
ExtBd **Arial**

ExtBdIta ***Arial***
LтCon Arial Condensed
Con Arial Condensed
BdCon **Arial Condensed**
ExtBdCon **Arial Condensed**

Bk ITC Avant Garde Gothic
BkObl *ITC Avant Garde Gothic*
Demi **ITC Avant Garde Gothic**
DemiObl ***ITC Avant Garde Gothic***
ExtLt AvantGarde Gothic
ExtLtObl *AvantGarde Gothic*
Med AvantGarde Gothic
MedObl *AvantGarde Gothic*
Bd **AvantGarde Gothic**
BdObl ***AvantGarde Gothic***
BkCon ITC Avant Garde Gothic
MedCon ITC Avant Garde Gothic
DemiCon **ITC Avant Garde Gothic**
BdCon **ITC Avant Garde Gothic**

Lт Avenir
LтObl *Avenir*
Reg Avenir
Obl *Avenir*
Hvy **Avenir**
HvyObl ***Avenir***
Bk Avenir
BkObl *Avenir*
Med Avenir
MedObl *Avenir*
Blk **Avenir**
BlkObl ***Avenir***

Reg Baskerville
Iта *Baskerville*
SemBd **Baskerville**
SemBdIta ***Baskerville***
Bd **Baskerville**
BdIta ***Baskerville***
ExpReg BASKERVILLE

Reg Bauer Bodoni
Iта *Bauer Bodoni*
Bd **Bauer Bodoni**
BdIta ***Bauer Bodoni***
Blk **Bauer Bodoni**
BlkIta ***Bauer Bodoni***

Reg Bell
Iта *Bell*
SemBd Bell
Bd **Bell**

Reg Bembo
Iта *Bembo*
Bd **Bembo**
BdIta ***Bembo***
SemBd Bembo
SemBdIta *Bembo*
ExtBd **Bembo**
ExtBdIta ***Bembo***
ExpReg BEMBO

Reg Bodoni
Iта *Bodoni*
Bd **Bodoni**
BdIta ***Bodoni***
PosBod **Bodoni**

Typeface listing

Bk Bodoni
BkIta *Bodoni*
PosBodIta **Bodoni**
PosBodCmp **Bodoni**
BdCon **Bodoni**
Lt ITC Bookman
LtIta *ITC Bookman*
Demi **ITC Bookman**
DemiIta ***ITC Bookman***
Med ITC Bookman
MedIta *ITC Bookman*
Bd **ITC Bookman**
BdIta ***ITC Bookman***
Reg Calisto
Ita *Calisto*
Bd **Calisto**
BdIta ***Calisto***
Reg Caslon 540
Ita *Caslon 540*
Reg Centaur
Ita *Centaur*
Bd **Centaur**
BdIta ***Centaur***
Reg Century Schoolbook
Ita *Century Schoolbook*
Bd **Century Schoolbook**
BdIta ***Century Schoolbook***
Reg Century Old Style
Ita *Century Old Style*
Bd **Century Old Style**
Reg Bitstream Charter

Ita *Bitstream Charter*
Blk **Bitstream Charter**
BlkIta ***Bitstream Charter***
Bd **Bitstream Charter**
BdIta ***Bitstream Charter***
Reg Clarion
Ita *Clarion*
Bd **Clarion**
Reg Concorde
Ita *Concorde*
Bd **Concorde**
BdIta ***Concorde***
Reg Corona
Ita *Corona*
Bd **Corona**
Reg Dante
Ita *Dante*
Bd **Dante**
BdIta ***Dante***
Reg Ehrhardt
Ita *Ehrhardt*
SemiBd **Ehrhardt**
SemiBdIta ***Ehrhardt***
ExpReg EHRHARDT
Reg Excelsior
Ita *Excelsior*
Bd **Excelsior**
Bk ITC Franklin Gothic
BkObl *ITC Franklin Gothic*
Demi **ITC Franklin Gothic**
DemiObl ***ITC Franklin Gothic***

Hvy **ITC Franklin Gothic**
HvyObl ***ITC Franklin Gothic***
Reg **ATF Franklin Gothic**
Con **ATF Franklin Gothic**
ExtCon **ATF Franklin Gothic**
45Lt Frutiger
46LtIta *Frutiger*
55Reg Frutiger
56Ita *Frutiger*
65Bd **Frutiger**
66BdIta ***Frutiger***
75Blk **Frutiger**
76BlkIta ***Frutiger***
UltBlk **Frutiger**
Lt Futura
LtObl *Futura*
Bk Futura
BkObl *Futura*
Bd **Futura**
BdObl ***Futura***
Med Futura
MedObl *Futura*
Hvy **Futura**
HvyObl ***Futura***
LtCon Futura
LtConObl *Futura*
MedCon Futura
MedConObl *Futura*
BdCon **Futura**
BdConObl ***Futura***
ExtBdCon **Futura**

128

ExtBd **Futura**	Bd Garamond (Monotype)	17 **Bureau Grotesque**
ExtBdObl **Futura**	ɔlta *Garamond (Monotype)*	37 **Bureau Grotesque**
Rom ITC Galliard	ExpReg GARAMOND	53 Bureau Grotesque
Ita *ITC Galliard*	Lt Gill Sans	79 **Bureau Grotesque**
Bd **ITC Galliard**	LtIta *Gill Sans*	Bd **Headline Bold**
BdIta *ITC Galliard*	Reg Gill Sans	Lt Helvetica
Blk **ITC Galliard**	Ita *Gill Sans*	LtObl *Helvetica*
BlkIta *ITC Galliard*	Bd **Gill Sans**	Blk **Helvetica**
Ult **ITC Galliard**	BdIta *Gill Sans*	BlkObl *Helvetica*
UltIta *ITC Galliard*	ExtBd **Gill Sans**	LtCon Helvetica
Reg Adobe Garamond	UltBd **Gill Sans**	LtConObl *Helvetica*
Ita *Adobe Garamond*	Con Gill Sans	Con Helvetica
SemBd **Adobe Garamond**	BdCon **Gill Sans**	ConObl *Helvetica*
SemBdIta *Adobe Garamond*	UltBdCon **Gill Sans**	BdCon **Helvetica**
Bd **Adobe Garamond**	55Reg Glypha	BdConObl *Helvetica*
BdIta *Adobe Garamond*	56Obl *Glypha*	BlkCon **Helvetica**
Exp ADOBE GARAMOND	65Bd **Glypha**	BlkConObl *Helvetica*
Alt ꞇầȶ (Adobe Garamond)	66BdObl *Glypha*	Reg **Helvetica Inserat**
AltIta *ȶꞇ* (Adobe Garamond)	35Thin Glypha	Compr **Helvetica**
Titling ADOBE GARAMOND	36ThinObl *Glypha*	ExtCompr **Helvetica**
Lt ITC Garamond	45Lt Glypha	UltCompr **Helvetica**
LtIta *ITC Garamond*	46LtObl *Glypha*	Reg Hollander
Bd **ITC Garamond**	75Blk **Glypha**	Ita *Hollander*
BdIta *ITC Garamond*	76BlkObl *Glypha*	Bd **Hollander**
Bk ITC Garamond	No126Lt Grotesque	Cap HOLLANDER
BkIta *ITC Garamond*	No126LtIta *Grotesque*	Reg Imprint
Ult **ITC Garamond**	No215Reg Grotesque	Ita *Imprint*
UltIta *ITC Garamond*	No215Ita *Grotesque*	Bd **Imprint**
Reg Garamond (Monotype)	No215Bd **Grotesque**	BdIta *Imprint*
Ita *Garamond (Monotype)*	13 **Bureau Grotesque**	Reg Ionic
OriginalIta *Garamond (Monotype)*	15 **Bureau Grotesque**	Ita *Ionic*

Bd **Ionic**	Bd **Lucida**	66MedIta *Neue Helvetica*
Reg Janson Text	BdIta *Lucida*	85Hvy **Neue Helvetica**
Ita *Janson Text*	Reg Lucida Sans	86HeavyIta ***Neue Helvetica***
Bd **Janson Text**	Ita *Lucida Sans*	25UltLt Neue Helvetica
BdIta ***Janson Text***	Bd **Lucida Sans**	26UltLtIta *Neue Helvetica*
SmCp JANSON TEXT	BdIta ***Lucida Sans***	95Blk **Neue Helvetica**
ItaOsf *Janson Text*	Reg Maximus	96BlkIta ***Neue Helvetica***
BdOsf **Janson Text**	Bk Mendoza	35Thin Neue Helvetica
BdItaOsf ***Janson Text***	BkIta *Mendoza*	36ThinIta *Neue Helvetica*
Reg Joanna	Bd **Mendoza**	55Reg Neue Helvetica
Ita *Joanna*	BdIta ***Mendoza***	56Ita *Neue Helvetica*
Bd **Joanna**	Reg Meridien	75Bd **Neue Helvetica**
BdIta ***Joanna***	Ita *Meridien*	76BdIta ***Neue Helvetica***
SemBd **Joanna**	Med Meridien	27UltLtCon Neue Helvetica
SemBdIta ***Joanna***	MedIta *Meridien*	28UltLtConObl *Neue Helvetica*
ExtBd **Joanna**	Bd **Meridien**	97BlackCon **Neue Helvetica**
Reg Life	BdIta ***Meridien***	98BlkConObl ***Neue Helvetica***
Ita *Life*	Reg Minion	107ExtBlkCon **Neue Helvetica**
Bd **Life**	Ita *Minion*	37ThinCon Neue Helvetica
45Lt Linotype Centennial	SemBd **Minion**	38ThinConObl *Neue Helvetica*
46LtIta *Linotype Centennial*	SemBdIta ***Minion***	57Con Neue Helvetica
55Reg Linotype Centennial	Bd **Minion**	58ConObl *Neue Helvetica*
56Ita *Linotype Centennial*	BdIta ***Minion***	77BdCon **Neue Helvetica**
65Bd **Linotype Centennial**	Blk **Minion**	78BdConObl ***Neue Helvetica***
66BdIta ***Linotype Centennial***	Exp MINION	47LtCon Neue Helvetica
75Blk **Linotype Centennial**	SwAsh *MINION*	48LtConObl *Neue Helvetica*
76BlkIta ***Linotype Centennial***	SwshMedIta *MINION*	67MedCon Neue Helvetica
LtSmCaps LINOTYPE CENTENNIAL	SwshDisplt *MINION*	68MedConObl *Neue Helvetica*
RegSmCaps LINOTYPE CENTENNIAL	45Lt Neue Helvetica	87HvyCon **Neue Helvetica**
Reg Lucida	46LtIta *Neue Helvetica*	88HvyConObl ***Neue Helvetica***
Ita *Lucida*	65Med **Neue Helvetica**	23UltLtExt Neue Helvetica

24UltLtExtObl Neue Helvetica
93BlkExt **Neue Helvetica**
94BlkExtObl ***Neue Helvetica***
33ThinExt Neue Helvetica
34ThinExtObl Neue Helvetica
53Ext Neue Helvetica
54ExtObl Neue Helvetica
73BdExt **Neue Helvetica**
74BdExtObl ***Neue Helvetica***
43LtExt Neue Helvetica
44LtExtObl Neue Helvetica
63MedExt Neue Helvetica
64MedExtObl Neue Helvetica
83HvyExt **Neue Helvetica**
84HvyExtObl ***Neue Helvetica***
Reg ITC New Baskerville
Ita *ITC New Baskerville*
Bd **ITC New Baskerville**
BdIta ***ITC New Baskerville***
Reg New Caledonia
RegIta *New Caledonia*
SemBd New Caledonia
Bd **New Caledonia**
BdIta *New Caledonia*
Blk **New Caledonia**
Reg New Century Schoolbook
Ita *New Century Schoolbook*
Bd **New Century Schoolbook**
BdIta ***New Century Schoolbk***
Reg News Gothic
Obl *News Gothic*

Bd **News Gothic**
BdObl ***News Gothic***
Reg News Plantin
Ita *News Plantin*
Bd **News Plantin**
BdIta ***News Plantin***
Reg Nimrod
Ita *Nimrod*
Bd **Nimrod**
BdIta ***Nimrod***
Bk ITC Officina Sans
BkIta *ITC Officina Sans*
Bd **ITC Officina Sans**
BdIta ***ITC Officina Sans***
Bk ITC Officina Serif
BkIta *ITC Officina Serif*
Bd **ITC Officina Serif**
BdIta ***ITC Officina Serif***
Reg Old Style
Ita *Old Style*
Bd **Old Style**
BdIta ***Old Style***
Rom Olympian
Ita *Olympian*
Bd **Olympian**
BdIta ***Olympian***
Reg Palatino
Ita *Palatino*
Bd **Palatino**
BdIta ***Palatino***
SmCp PALATINO

Reg Perpetua
Ita *Perpetua*
Bd **Perpetua**
BdIta ***Perpetua***
TitlingReg PERPETUA
Reg Photina
Ita *Photina*
Bd **Photina**
BdIta ***Photina***
SemBd Photina
SemBdIta *Photina*
UltBd **Photina**
UltBdIta ***Photina***
Reg Plantin
Ita *Plantin*
Bd **Plantin**
BdIta ***Plantin***
Lt Plantin
LtIta *Plantin*
SemBd **Plantin**
SemBdIta *Plantin*
BdCon **Plantin**
ExpReg PLANTIN
Reg Sabon
Ita *Sabon*
Bd **Sabon**
BdIta ***Sabon***
SmCp SABON
Reg FF Scala
Ita *FF Scala*
Bd **FF Scala**

131

Typeface listing

Caps FF Scala	Bd **Swift**	66BdObl *Univers*
45Lt Serifa	ExtBd **Swift**	75Blk **Univers**
46LtIta *Serifa*	Reg Swift	76BlkObl **Univers**
55Rom Serifa	Ita *Swift*	47ConLt Univers
56Ita *Serifa*	BdCon **Swift**	48ConLtObl *Univers*
65Bd **Serifa**	Reg Syntax	57Con Univers
75Blk **Serifa**	Ita *Syntax*	58ConObl *Univers*
Reg Stempel Garamond	Bd **Syntax**	67ConBd **Univers**
Ita *Stempel Garamond*	Blk **Syntax**	68ConBdObl **Univers**
Bd **Stempel Garamond**	UltBlk **Syntax**	85ExtBlk **Univers**
BdIta ***Stempel Garamond***	Reg Times New Roman	86ExtBlkObl **Univers**
Reg ITC Stone Informal	Ita *Times New Roman*	53Exp Univers
Ita *ITC Stone Informal*	Bd **Times New Roman**	54ExpObl *Univers*
SemBd **ITC Stone Informal**	BdIta ***Times New Roman***	63BdExt **Univers**
SemBdIta ***ITC Stone Informal***	ExpReg TIMES NEW ROMAN	64BdExtObl **Univers**
Bd **ITC Stone Informal**	SemBd Times New Roman	73BlkExt **Univers**
BdIta ***ITC Stone Informal***	SemBdIta *Times New Roman*	74BlkExtObl **Univers**
Reg ITC Stone Sans	ExtBd **Times New Roman**	83ExtBlkEx **Univers**
Ita *ITC Stone Sans*	Reg Times Sm Text	84ExBkExOb **Univers**
SemBd **ITC Stone Sans**	Ita *Times Sm Text*	Reg Utopia
SemBdIta ***ITC Stone Sans***	Bd **Times Sm Text**	Ita *Utopia*
Bd **ITC Stone Sans**	Reg Trump Mediaeval	SemBd **Utopia**
BdIta ***ITC Stone Sans***	Ita *Trump Mediaeval*	SemBdIta ***Utopia***
Reg ITC Stone Serif	Bd **Trump Mediaeval**	Bd **Utopia**
Ita *ITC Stone Serif*	BdIta ***Trump Mediaeval***	BdIta ***Utopia***
SemBd **ITC Stone Serif**	SmCp TRUMP MEDIAEVAL	Blk **Utopia**
SemBdIta ***ITC Stone Serif***	45Lt Univers	Exp UTOPIA
Bd **ITC Stone Serif**	46LtObl *Univers*	Titling UTOPIA
BdIta ***ITC Stone Serif***	55Reg Univers	Reg Monotype Walbaum
Lt Swift	56Obl *Univers*	Ita *Monotype Walbaum*
LtIta *Swift*	65Bd **Univers**	Med **Monotype Walbaum**

Typeface index

Typeface index

General index

When there is more than one reference, turn to the page number in **bold** for the most concise definition.

General index